DIETRICH BONHOEFFER
Follower of the Living Jesus

AN AUTHENTIC EVANGELICAL APPRECIATION

Michael T. Hayes

WITH FOREWORD BY JOHN W. MATTHEWS

Lutheran University Press
Minneapolis, Minnesota

Dietrich Bonhoeffer: Follower of the Living Jesus
AN AUTHENTIC EVANGELICAL APPRECIATION
by Michael T. Hayes

Copyright 2018 Charlot A. Hayes. All rights reserved. Published by Lutheran University Press, an imprint of 1517 Media. No part of this publication may be reproduced, stored in a retrieval system, or transmitted in any form or by any means, electronic, mechanical, photocopying, recording, or otherwise, without prior permission of the publisher.

ISBN 978-1-942304-31-9
eISBN 978-1-942304-52-4

DEDICATION

Ray S. Anderson
Pastor, Professor, Friend.
Ray so imbibed the faith of Dietrich Bonhoeffer
that knowing him was itself an introduction
to the mind and heart of Bonhoeffer.
Like Bonhoeffer, Ray read, spoke, and lived Scripture
with a fresh vision and solid integrity.

A family portrait shows all eight Bonhoeffer children gathered around their mother in 1911 or 12. Dietrich is the blond boy standing with his arm on the table.

Table of Contents

Foreword 7

From the Author 11

Introduction 13

CHAPTER ONE
Childhood and Youth 23
    Family and Childhood 23
    Youth and Education 27
    Early Career 31

CHAPTER TWO
Time of Great Change 43
    New York 43
    Berlin 46
        Creation and Fall 47
        Christ the Center 53
        Thy Kingdom Come 60

CHAPTER THREE
The Rise of Hitler and the Nazis 66
    Germany after the War 66
    The Appointment of Hitler 67
    The Church and the Jewish Question 71
    The Bethel Confession and the Confessing Church ... 73
    A Pastoral Call 76
    The Barmen Declaration of 1934 77
    Contemporizing New Testament Texts 78
    Three Personal Letters 81

CHAPTER FOUR
The Seminary at Finkenwalde 90
    The Seminary 90
    Discipleship 94
    Life Together 104

CHAPTER FIVE
Conspiracy and Engagement 116
- Disintegration of the Confessing Church 116
- The Collective Pastorates 118
- Travel to America and Back Again 120
- Conspiracy Understood as Patriotism 122
- Engagement to Maria 124

CHAPTER SIX
Ethics 128

CHAPTER SEVEN
Letters and Papers from Prison 143
- The Early Letters 143
- The Theological Letters 144
- Execution 168

CHAPTER EIGHT
Conclusion 173

EPILOGUE
Germany after the War 180

APPENDIX ONE
Timeline 189

APPENDIX TWO
A Brief Bonhoeffer Bibliography 192

About the Author 197

Foreword

Today one can pick up any number of biographies, short or long, about the life and legacy of Dietrich Bonhoeffer. From the first—and arguably definitive—biography by Eberhard Bethge in 1967, to other subsequent works by Bosanquet, Glazener, Metaxas, Schlingsensiepen, Marsh, Tietz, or Reynolds, many have striven to make the story of Dietrich Bonhoeffer known to the world. Impressive videos by Trinity Films, Journey Films, and YouTube have been created; numerous articles and website entries also attempt to offer glimpses of this twentieth century witness to Jesus Christ.

Dietrich Bonhoeffer's life spanned the first half of the twentieth century, a period including both world wars, the Russian Revolution, an Armenian genocide, and a world-wide economic depression. Born into an upper-middle-class German family of significant cultural, scientific, and ecclesiastical influence, Bonhoeffer enjoyed a dual career of academic theology and pastoral ministry. Completing his doctoral degree at the age of twenty-one, he became a vicar, foreign exchange student, chaplain, and university teaching assistant. Early in the days of Germany's National Socialist regime, he was a vocal opponent of the vision being put forward by Adolf Hitler. Bonhoeffer was critically supportive of the famous Barmen Declaration (1934) of the nascent Confessing Church, to which he was asked a year later to serve as the director of one of its preacher seminaries. For slightly over two years he prepared young pastors to serve congregations that were identified as opposed to the theology and practice of the German Christian (Nazified) state Church. It was in the fall of 1937, when Bonhoeffer's seminary was closed by the Gestapo, that he contemplated resistance in alternative ways. It was at this time that he learned in greater detail through his brother-in-law of the secret plans within military intelligence for the overthrow of Nazi leadership, including plans for the assassination of the Führer. Ultimately, Dietrich Bonhoeffer was employed to work for military intelligence (the *Abwehr*), making use of his international church contacts to garner sympathy for the resistors and support for a future Germany without Hitler. His four-year clandestine labor for the conspiracy ended with his arrest, followed by two years of imprisonment and finally his death by hanging on April 9, 1945. It was his tragic death and life sacrifice for truth and justice that, more than anything, has occasioned a retrieval of his profound, ambitious and controversial literary legacy. His dear friend and colleague, Eberhard Bethge, was entrusted with the remains (*Nachlass*) of his writings and correspondence; since 1945, sixteen volumes of material (the *Dietrich Bonhoeffer Works*) have been assembled, edited, and made available for study and inspiration.

One of the unique and significant aspects of Dietrich Bonhoeffer's life is that inspiration from his legacy is appreciated by persons from a wide spectrum of religious convictions, even some with no religious commitment. Conservative and evangelical Christians most often embrace *Discipleship* and *Life Together*, while more liberal-minded Christians, and non-Christians, find his *Ethics* and *Letters and Papers from Prison* most attractive. An intriguing part of Bonhoeffer's legacy is this appeal to persons of significantly different perspectives. The multifarious character of his writings has occasioned more than a few people emphasizing (hijacking?) one particular aspect, while minimizing or even denying other dialectical and complimentary aspects.

Michael Hayes, a self-professing evangelical, offers in this volume perhaps the first—and only—biography that shows how Dietrich Bonhoeffer's life and legacy can be of great inspiration to evangelicals, while not diminishing or dismissing his (Bonhoeffer's) "liberal" theological, ethical and social commitments. Hayes understands Bonhoeffer's contribution to address key concerns for evangelicals: scripture, salvation, sin, Jesus Christ, church, and world. He argues — throughout this biography — that for Dietrich Bonhoeffer, the Bible had immense authority (a primary evangelical commitment) while he simultaneously avoided a fundamentalist hermeneutic. For Dietrich Bonhoeffer, ever the Lutheran, Jesus Christ is unquestionably the incarnate Word of God, present in preaching, community, and sacraments, at the center of the church, history, nature, and individual lives. Hayes, an evangelical, challenges fellow evangelicals not to diminish Bonhoeffer's importance for lacking an emphasis on a "private" experience of conversion, as understood by American evangelicals. Finally, Hayes affirms Bonhoeffer's dialectical grasp of the "Word and World," while not succumbing to a heretical Manichaean dualism, often a risk and dark side of evangelical preaching and teaching.

So why is this book, addressed primarily to evangelicals, published under the imprint of Lutheran University Press? Why is this book, authored by a Covenant pastor, edited and enthusiastically endorsed by a Lutheran pastor/theologian? For very intentional reasons! Within many Christian denominations reside a spectrum of pieties and theological orientations; for sure, particular denominations tend to have more of one type than its opposite. In fact, most mainline Christian congregations have evangelically-minded persons in their ranks. Within the Evangelical Lutheran Church in America (ELCA), a decidedly mainline denomination, are persons with clearly evangelical commitments. And so, an "authentic evangelical appreciation" of Bonhoeffer's legacy is in order. Michael Hayes offers here a challenging apologetic of Bonhoeffer's liberal ideas that evangelicals ought to consider, just as it simultaneously offers helpful evangelical ideas that more liberal-minded people ought to consider. This creative—yet faithful—symbiosis is the beauty of Hayes' effort.

To date, Bonhoeffer's appeal to evangelical Christians has often involved a selective use of his texts, combined with a distorted interpretation of his political/social actions. Michael Hayes presents an accurate contextual portrayal of Bonhoeffer's texts with an authentic interpretation of his actions. Hopefully, evangelical Christians will appreciate one of their own who has spent four decades of prayerful engagement, scholarly discernment, and ongoing "conversation" with Dietrich Bonhoeffer, and here offers a masterful tome about this contemporary witness to Jesus Christ. In *Dietrich Bonhoeffer: Follower of the Living Jesus*, the life story of Bonhoeffer is told in a way that evangelicals can—hopefully—hear and respect, without distortion or domestication. Michael Hayes has gifted the church of Jesus Christ with a unique and marvelous gift that can instruct and inspire disciples in the third millennium who seek to be "followers of the living Jesus."

> John W. Matthews
> *Pastor of Grace Lutheran Church of Apple Valley, Minnesota*
> *Adjunct instructor of religion at Augsburg University, Minneapolis*
> *Past-president of the International Bonhoeffer Society—*
>   *English Language Section*

The Bonhoeffer family making music together.
Dietrich is playing the piano.

From the Author

The text contains many footnotes because it is hoped that reader will want to pursue Bonhoeffer studies in greater detail. A large portion of those notes, however, refer to just two sources: Eberhard Bethge's biography of Bonhoeffer, in a revised and greatly expanded edition in 2000, and the seventeen volume *Dietrich Bonhoeffer Works in English*. To minimize distraction, these books are noted within the text as "*DB*," followed by page number, and "*DBWE,*" followed by volume and page number. Some books, such as C. S. Lewis' *Mere Christianity*, have appeared in so many editions and printings that I only cite the chapter, not the page, from which a quotation is taken.

For Bonhoeffer's better known works there are several translations and editions. All quotations here are from *DBWE*. This will present some problems for those who do not have access to the set but there seems no practical way to avoid the difficulty.

Second, with some frustration I have chosen to use masculine pronouns when speaking of God. I know and appreciate the purpose of inclusive language in our day. Inclusive language is used in the English edition of *Dietrich Bonhoeffer Works*, where it sometimes makes for some very awkward readings. I have chosen biblical familiarity over awkwardness, though I will not defend my choice with vigor.

Third, in simplest terms, the purpose of this book is to encourage the reader to look more carefully, more deeply, more insightfully into the foundations laid for us in Scripture. We want to look more intensely at our own traditions, not to see whether we want to change traditions. To an unhealthy degree, we have become locked into a set of answers developed mostly in the nineteenth century. We have forgotten that questions are important. Without a question, answers make little sense. If I teach you that the answer is 49, you will have gained nothing unless you know the question is "What is 7 x 7?"

Finally, gratitude is wonderfully humbling. My gratitude for all their help with this book extends to many friends, including our local Bonhoeffer Society in Red Wing, Minnesota. Most of all, however, my thanks are given to Pastor John Matthews, who took up the task of encourager and got more than he bargained for by becoming the editor. There are no words to express the depth of my gratitude.

And of course, in a more general sense, I am grateful to my wife, Char, for believing in me, nudging me, and helping me in countless ways far beyond this book.

INTRODUCTION

Building on Biblical Foundations

*May God lead us kindly through these times,
but above all, may God lead us to himself.*[1]

More than any theologian since Martin Luther, Dietrich Bonhoeffer's life and his writings are so intertwined that we cannot effectively study one without the other. Those who are first turning to a study of Bonhoeffer's legacy are often surprised that nearly every book and article about him includes a biography, however brief.

This book is no exception. My intent is to show that the orthodox foundations of modern evangelicalism are the same foundations we find in Dietrich Bonhoeffer's theology. Bonhoeffer, however, builds a mature body of thought on those foundations which leaves most of us evangelicals looking like naive little children.

The result could be called a "theological biography" or perhaps a "biographical theology."[2] Whichever this book may be, my hope is that the reader may come to appreciate Bonhoeffer as a person, as a theologian, and as a follower of the living Jesus.

Why are we interested in Dietrich Bonhoeffer? After all, he was a German intellectual in an age and culture far different from our own. He never got firmly established in any career, though he was drawn both to the university and the church. He was only one among millions who died during World War II. He was somewhat exceptional because he was executed for his affiliation in a plot to assassinate Hitler, but so were hundreds of others and, at any rate, his role in the conspiracy was both minor and unsuccessful.

Yet, Dietrich Bonhoeffer is of growing importance for many. Biographies are still being written and are popular. His entire corpus, down to the most minor letters to his friends,[3] has now been published in both German and English.

What makes Bonhoeffer of even greater importance now than in his own day?

Those who like to read biographies find Bonhoeffer's story fascinating. He was born into an extraordinary family, showed great intellectual acumen even as a youth, worked to undermine the Nazis, spoke and wrote with unusual depth in theology and spirituality. In the end, he was hanged for his complicity in the conspiracy to assassinate Hitler. He was an answer to the challenge Carl Sandburg had given to the wild evangelist Billy Sunday in 1915: "I ask you to come through and show me where you're pouring out the blood of your life."[4]

Those who read history find that Bonhoeffer's life in Germany provides an excellent window to gain insight into what it was like to be German in the midst of a catastrophic cultural and moral upheaval. By following Bonhoeffer's story, we begin to understand Hitler's dominance of parliament, university, and church, three of his earliest and most consequential conquests. Bonhoeffer's experiences help us to see how hard it was for the German people, especially the German Jews, to resist the power and terror of Adolf Hitler.

Those who want to explore theology find Bonhoeffer important because of the creative way he built upon biblical foundations, because of what he resisted in contemporary theologies, and because of the strength of his intellectual integrity. He spoke truth with such directness that we still find his thinking to be a bracing challenge.

Adding to all this, we find Bonhoeffer fascinating because we cannot easily categorize him. He was a living set of paradoxes. Bonhoeffer was a German Lutheran yet he was drawn to the Swiss Reformed theologian Karl Barth. He was grounded in the twin foundations of Pietism—devotion to Jesus Christ and a deep trust in Scripture—while being skeptical of Pietism. He strongly resisted much (but certainly not all) of the theological liberalism of his day but found nothing of interest in fundamentalism. His personality was marked by the stereotypical German reserve, yet during his year of study in the United States, he was delighted by the emotional depth of worship he found in the black church, particularly at Abyssinian Baptist Church in New York City.[5]

Because he fits few of our preconceived categories, no one can lay claim to him and say, "He was just like us." He wasn't quite like any of us.

Speaking personally, I dwell on Bonhoeffer for all those reasons, yet what most makes the man so important to me is something much simpler. Stephen Fowl and L. Gregory Jones comment that, "Unless Christians embody their interpretation of Scripture (thus producing a certain character), their interpretation is in vain."[6] Bonhoeffer, they insist, is a perfect example of one who reads Scripture in a character-reforming way. Yes! *I read Bonhoeffer because he has so very much to teach me about being a follower of Jesus Christ and a person of the Word.*

More specifically, why do we who have thought of ourselves as evangelicals listen to Dietrich Bonhoeffer? What has he to say to us? Was he an evangelical himself? I will spend little time addressing these questions directly. I simply want to express my own way of reading Bonhoeffer through a biblical perspective. This is not meant to be a book *about* Bonhoeffer and evangelicals but a book about Bonhoeffer *by* an evangelical *for* fellow evangelicals.

Writing anything about Bonhoeffer is difficult because there is so much material to cover and it is all so deeply intertwined that it is almost impossible to separate out just one idea from its greater context. Writing about Bonhoeffer for an evangelical reader is even more difficult because in my own lifetime the word "evangelical" has undergone so many transformations that I am ready to throw it out the window as a now-useless term. I have thought of myself as an evangelical for more than half a century, but now I am content merely to say I want to be a biblical follower of Jesus Christ. It is not that I have changed so much as that the word "evangelical" now conjures up quite different meanings.

Broadly speaking, an evangelical—in the older sense—is a person who believes in the Bible as the Word of God, taking its plain sense as authoritative whenever possible and, primarily on that biblical basis, trusts Jesus Christ as the living Son of God, Lord, and Savior. There are within evangelicalism, of course, a great many variations on these themes. I confess I have little in common with those who the secular journalists call evangelical these days, especially when speaking of political conservatives.

For the most part, evangelicalism is an Anglo-American phenomenon. Though extensive evangelical missionary service has been extended around the globe, its influence has been minimal in continental Europe. The church in Germany in the first half of the twentieth century was divided almost exclusively into Roman Catholic and Lutheran/Reformed factions, with Anabaptists, Pietists, and sects such as Jehovah's Witnesses being very small minorities in whom Bonhoeffer showed no interest. "*Evangelische*" in that German context essentially meant "Protestant."

When he spent the 1930-31 school year in America, Bonhoeffer found a great gulf between fundamentalist and liberal churches. Prohibition and the infamous Scopes Trial of 1927[7] had become occasions for the humiliation of the fundamentalists. Liberalism became dominant in the American churches, especially those called "mainline," and would remain so for another half century or more.

In the years after the Second World War a certain *via media* arose between liberalism and fundamentalism in America. The Left in its more extreme forms seems to have had more questions than answers and the Right tended to have rigid answers with little room for questions. The mark of a fundamentalist mindset is an insecure clinging to answers in theology and rules in ethics. The evangelicals, seeking a middle ground, have tended to have faith and a few questions, too.

Schools like Fuller Seminary in California (my own school), Bethel in Minnesota, Trinity in Illinois, and Gordon-Conwell in Massachusetts have all sought to be true to orthodox Christianity while taking seriously the academic requirement that Bible and theology need to be examined afresh in every generation. Leaders such as John Stott, N. T. Wright, and Eugene Peterson, each in their own unique way, have laid careful biblical foundations for their work while avoiding fundamentalism's rigid biblicism.

In more recent years, as American secular journalists have taken an interest in the conservative Christian movement, the word "evangelical" has undergone another shift and is now little distinguished from fundamentalism or even mere political conservatism.

Bonhoeffer shares with evangelicals two foundational convictions: that Jesus Christ is Lord and that the Bible is the Word of God. His commitment to Christ and Scripture was formed in a cultural and religious context quite unlike anything we have experienced, so of course he would express and emphasize some things differently than we might. However, no one can doubt the clarity and depth of his devotion to Jesus Christ or the hunger he had to hear the Spirit of Jesus Christ in and through Scripture.

Less evident in Bonhoeffer's thought is the conviction that Jesus Christ is the personal Savior of the repentant sinner, though the unspoken idea permeates nearly everything he said.[8] In this, as in other ways, he seems influenced by a negative opinion of the German Pietists, whom he saw as being too demonstrative, too obsessed with their own individual relationship with Jesus Christ and their own "testimonies," and too little engaged with the broader world. He would not have called himself "born again" in an American revivalist sense.

Bonhoeffer built a theological house on biblical foundations that does not look at all like the evangelical culture and subcultures in America today. He matured beyond his beginnings (without ever abandoning them), while we evangelicals have tended to remain beginners in the Christian life.

Before looking at the life of Bonhoeffer, it may be helpful to examine this theme of maturity from a biblical perspective so that we will recognize what Bonhoeffer has in the back of his mind. We'll look at the matter with some care because it is a solidly biblical idea that was very important to Bonhoeffer but of little interest to most conservative Christians.

We remind ourselves often that Jesus said we must become like children to enter the kingdom of heaven (Matthew 18:3), but seldom do we speak of his admonition. "Be perfect, therefore, as your heavenly Father is perfect" (Matthew 5:48). The word translated "perfect" is the Greek word *teleios*, which means complete or fulfillment of purpose. We are perfect when we have become all our Creator has intended us to be, when we have fulfilled God's purpose in creation.

Frequently *teleios* connotes maturity. "Brothers and sisters, do not be children in your thinking," wrote Paul, "rather, be infants in evil but in thinking be adults (*teleios*)" (1 Corinthians 14:20). To the Colossians, Paul explained his purpose in ministry: "It is [Christ] whom we proclaim, warning everyone and teaching everyone in all wisdom, so that we may present everyone mature (*teleios*) in Christ" (Colossians 1:28).

More expansively, we find this in Ephesians:

> The gifts he gave were that some would be apostles, some prophets, some evangelists, some pastors and teachers, to equip the saints for the work of ministry, for building up the body of Christ, until all of us come to the unity of the faith and of the knowledge of the Son

of God, to *maturity* (*teleios*), to the measure of the full stature of Christ. We must no longer be children, tossed to and fro and blown about by every wind of doctrine, by people's trickery, by their craftiness in deceitful scheming. But speaking the truth in love, we must grow up in every way into him who is the head, into Christ, from whom the whole body, joined and knit together by every ligament with which it is equipped, as each part is working properly, promotes the body's growth in building itself up in love (Ephesians 4:11-16, emphasis added).

James, that great enemy of those who would use grace as a way of evading responsibility for their own lives, encouraged his readers to "let endurance have its full (*teleios*) effect, so that you may be mature (*teleios*) and complete, lacking in nothing" (James 1:4). And John, the model of gentleness, taught that "There is no fear in love, but perfect (*teleios*) love casts out fear; for fear has to do with punishment, and whoever fears has not reached perfection (*teleios*) in love" (1 John 4:18). Look, too, at 1 Corinthians 3:1-3 and Hebrews 5:11-14.

Eugene Peterson notes our arrested development when he writes, "Surveyed as a whole, we are immersed in probably the most immature and mindless religion, ranging from infantile to adolescent, that any culture has ever witnessed."[9] It is as if the church, a major force in the shaping of the American character, grew so satisfied with how "Christian" America had become that it simply stopped working, stopped contributing, and began entrusting itself to the culture. The parent prematurely let the child become the leader of the family.

We must grow up in every way into Christlikeness of character in order to fulfill the creation as *imago dei*, the image of God. We cannot fulfill God's intention for us without growing up to become mature and Christlike in character. Bonhoeffer will challenge us to do just that. He was not content to remain immature, to rely on pat answers, to be bound by unexamined conventions.

Dietrich Bonhoeffer, I am sure, would be very ill at ease in a twenty-first century evangelical church and would speak strongly against our self-imposed immaturity, our self-satisfaction, our tendency to look down on those who differ from us, our shallow understanding of Scripture and theology, and our insulation from the injustices of the world around us. Historian Mark Noll noted several years ago, "The trouble with the evangelical mind is that there is not much of an evangelical mind."[10] To Bonhoeffer the evangelical neglect of loving God *with the whole mind*[11] would be utterly inexcusable.

There are, it seems to me, at least three areas in which we modern American evangelicals would be a disappointment to Bonhoeffer.

First, we have little spiritual depth and even look with suspicion on the more Catholic tradition of spiritual formation. Thanks to the work of Richard Foster, Dallas Willard, Eugene Peterson, Henry Nouwen, and others, spiritual formation is becoming an area of growth for us.

Second, we have tended to value answers more than questions and so have let our minds stagnate into a small pond of pat answers. Those pat answers have become little more than cliches because they are answers to questions we no longer ask. We dismiss or even flee from anyone who raises questions and seeks new levels of understanding. We simply want to hear the old, old story again and again.

Third, about a century ago we became confused about the relationship between church and culture. The Scopes Trial humiliated conservatives, and the failure of Prohibition discouraged us. We had been leaders in working for social justice and in serving the poor (e.g., Salvation Army, homeless shelters, the Young Men's Christian Association and the Young Women's Christian Association), but suddenly felt like outsiders in our own culture. It was that sense of humiliation and embarrassment that caused the American evangelicals to step back from roles of leadership in serving the poor and social justice issues. Years later, Jerry Falwell and the "Moral Majority" made an attempt at changing our place in American society but were too aligned with a particular brand of conservative politics to speak clearly for the Gospel.

There has developed in some circles a distinct, isolated mentality. One need only walk into a Christian bookstore or, even more dramatic, tune into the television channel Trinity Broadcasting Network to see how separated this mentality is from reality. They have constructed their own little world, often gaudy and always self-centered. I feel horrified seeing this mentality until I remind myself that it is only by the grace of God that I am allowed into the Kingdom. I need to occupy myself with saying *thank you* rather than with judging those unlike me.

In recent years evangelicalism has been marked by another trend: the megachurch. These are almost always newly-formed congregations that have begun with an ambitious vision to become large.

While some may have sacrificed the Gospel for the sake of popularity (such as those who preach that the Good News is nothing more than God wanting to make us each happy—and perhaps wealthy), others are finding creative avenues to articulate an authentic Gospel in ways that communicate well with those new to the church, those who are sometimes called seekers.

Yet, for all our varieties and shortcomings, we evangelicals have remained firmly committed to the core of our faith: Scripture and the Lord Jesus Christ. Dietrich Bonhoeffer expands the edges of our understanding not because he doubted or was dissatisfied with this core but because he was so very certain of that core. And, most deeply, he was very confident in the One who stands at the center, the Creator who is known in the Spirit of Jesus Christ. What makes Bonhoeffer unlike many conservative Christians is that he places the priority not on the doctrines of Christ and Scripture but on the living, present reality of the Spirit of Jesus Christ.

If we share Bonhoeffer's confidence in Jesus Christ we, too, can follow his lead in moving beyond the basics into a mature faith. There will be some challenges along the way, for Dietrich Bonhoeffer is truly more of a challenge than a comfort to American evangelicals.

May we accept that challenge with grace and integrity.

Endnotes

1 Bonhoeffer's letter of 21 July 1944 was written one day after the failure of the most significant assassination attempt. Though we cannot know for sure, it is likely as he wrote these words, he suspected that he would not leave prison alive.

2 "Indeed, what continues to make Bonhoeffer so widely known, admired, read, and studied is his unique *combination* of innovative theology and committed living" (Stephen Haynes, *The Bonhoeffer Phenomenon*, Minneapolis: Fortress Press, 2004, 9).

3 It is amazing that hundreds of his personal letters were so treasured by the recipients that they were saved.

4 Carl Sandburg, poem entitled *To a Contemporary Bunkshooter*, 1915. Sandburg's central complaint was that Sunday, a calculating manipulator, simply wasn't like Jesus.

5 It is fascinating that Bonhoeffer found the American seminary insufficiently intellectual and the American pulpit too intellectual. Clifford Green, one of the foremost Bonhoeffer scholars of our day, wrote of Bonhoeffer's American

experience: "Having made scathing criticisms of lectures pretending to be sermons in white churches, he warmed to the unfamiliar but authentic and moving preaching at Abyssinian." Here Bonhoeffer wrote, "I heard the gospel preached in the Negro churches. . . . Here one really could still hear someone talk in a Christian sense about sin and grace and the love of God and ultimate hope, albeit in a form different from that to which we are accustomed" (*DBWE* 10:30).

6   Stephen E. Fowl and L. Gregory Jones, *Reading in Communion: Scripture & Ethics in Christian Life* (Grand Rapids: Wm. B. Eerdmans Publishing Co., 1991, 85.

7   In 1927, school teacher John Scopes was tried and convicted of teaching evolution in his classes. The trial was of great national interest and excitement, with its outcomes leaving fundamentalists open to a very great deal of public ridicule. They became the target of many jokes about rejecting their ancestry, the monkeys, as well as rejecting science and its methodology.

8   The matter of individual salvation will come up in Chapter Six.

9   Eugene Peterson, *Under the Unpredictable Plant* (Wm. B. Eerdmans Publishing Co., 1992), 36.

10 Mark Noll, *The Scandal of the Evangelical Mind* (Wm. B. Eerdmans Publishing Co., 1994), 3.

11 Mark 12:28ff. Notice that the original statement in Deuteronomy 6 speaks of loving God with heart, soul, and strength. Jesus added the reference to the mind.

Dietrich Bonhoeffer
and his twin sister, Sabine

CHAPTER ONE

Childhood And Youth[1]

" . . . a proud awareness of being called to high responsibility in public service, intellectual achievement and leadership, and a deep-rooted obligation to be guardians of a great historical heritage and intellectual tradition."[2]

Dietrich Bonhoeffer knew from the beginning that Adolf Hitler was the enemy of all that was good about Germany. Even before Hitler was granted the position of Chancellor, which he defined for himself as a position with dictatorial powers, Bonhoeffer was preparing a radio message in which he disparaged the "Führer principle," the idea that Germany needed a strong leader who would simply take over the government, solve Germany's many problems, and receive unquestioning loyalty from his citizen subjects.[3]

Bonhoeffer knew that people desired such a leader because that would give them the illusion that they were relieved of responsibility. An acceptance of responsibility was fundamental to the character and thought of Bonhoeffer, whether in politics, theology, or ethics.[4]

To understand how Bonhoeffer could have been so prescient, we need to dwell first on the family in which he was raised. It was an extraordinary family[5] and all its members recognized from the beginning what a dangerous man Hitler was.

Family And Childhood

The sixth of eight children, Dietrich was born only minutes before his twin sister, Sabine, on February 4, 1906. His father, Karl, was an eminent psychiatrist who had little use for Freud or Jung because they simply were not scientific enough to meet his exacting standards for evidence. He had little interest in theories or intuitions. The children learned from their father to carefully examine even the most commonly accepted cliches, to think for themselves and to speak their minds with boldness and integrity. Karl raised a family of intelligent and articulate children. He was tolerant of error but impatient with carelessness in the children's thinking. Raised in this manner, Dietrich was led to the characteristics that would give his mature writing a freshness that can be very challenging.

Always in love with his wife Paula, Karl Bonhoeffer was devoted to his family, though of course with that usual German reserve in showing emotion. Nonetheless, there was clearly a romantic side to him. Paula von Hase seems to have won the heart of Karl Bonhoeffer the very first time they saw each other.

> I met a blond, blue-eyed girl who so captivated me the moment I entered the room by her free natural manner, her open uninhibited gaze, that my impression of this moment when I first saw my future wife remains in my memory as an almost mystical one that determined my life.[6]

Freud couldn't challenge Karl's scientific rationalism, but obviously Paula could!

Paula herself had come from a remarkable family of scholars and musicians. Her father was a noted professor of church history. She had an uncle and great-uncle (the Counts von Kalckreuth) who were well-known artists and whose paintings still hang in many museums and public places in Germany. Her mother had studied piano with Clara Schumann and Franz Lizst and had passed along to Paula a great love of music. This in turn was passed on to the Bonhoeffer children, for whom music was a natural part of every day in the family. Dietrich himself was such a good pianist that it was thought for a time he might become a concert artist.

Paula laid the foundations for Dietrich's spiritual health. She openly, consistently, and daily shared her faith in God with her children. Except for sending them to confirmation classes, Paula never expected the church to inculcate faith in her children. Faith development was a family task.

Having spent several months at Herrnhut[7] when she was younger, Paula had a relationship with God much like classical Pietism: deeply personal and foundational for all of life, centered on Scripture and on Jesus Christ. She showed little interest in the Lutheran church which, though rooted in the German psyche, was no longer a part of daily life for most people. That only about five percent of German Lutherans were active in the life of the church tells us more about the church, of course, than about their faith or Paula's. For the most part, especially in Berlin, the German Lutheran church seemed a lifeless shell which attracted very few Germans on any given Sunday.

The distinction which Bonhoeffer observed between the living faith of his mother and the lifeless liturgies of the Protestant churches in Germany had a significant impact on him. "There was no place for false piety or bogus religiosity in our home," writes Sabine.[8] As a young man Dietrich was careful to distinguish between the claims of the institutional church on one's life—claims for which he had little use—and the singular claim of Jesus Christ on the totality of one's being. Eventually he did come to think highly of the church but then, as a more mature man, he could dare to envision a "religionless" life of faith, not without the church but with a very different kind of church.

The governess and teacher for the younger children in the family were sisters, Kathe and Maria Horn. Both were Moravian Brethren. Though Paula reserved for herself the right to provide religious instruction for the children, the sisters were loved and respected by the children and must have been very effective examples of a life of faith.

His younger sister Susanne tells a delightful story of Dietrich's childhood faith:

> One day when we "three little ones" no longer slept in the same room, he declared to me and my sister Sabine, "During the day we think much too little about the dear Lord, and evenings after praying, I too think immediately about something else again and hear how you in the next room begin to chatter. Shall I, when in the evening the dear Lord comes to my mind, rap to you three times on the wall so that you too think about him?" Three raps on the wall—sometimes I can still hear them.[9]

Clearly, young Dietrich had already felt a deep connection with God at a very early age and was as intent upon developing that love as he was about all his pursuits as both a child and an adult.

There are two other strong qualities learned in the Bonhoeffer home. One was simple curiosity. There were always books to read and discuss, plays to be written and performed, songs to be sung, pets to be fed and cleaned, nature to be explored. Only the number of hours in a day seemed to limit the ways in which the Bonhoeffer children could be engaged in discovering and enjoying the world around them. Paula Bonhoeffer encouraged all this and "regarded mistakes as more forgivable than boredom" (*DB* 18).

Justice also was a profound value in the family. They had a deep sense of right and wrong, one to be espoused, the other not merely avoided but actively opposed. Truth must be told. "Dishonesty and fibbing," writes Bethge, "were severely punished; in comparison, broken windows and torn clothes hardly counted" (*DB* 19). One's duty must be done and done well.

Much of the idea of virtue in the family derived from their heritage. They were the fruit of generations of good, strong community leaders. "The rich world of his ancestors set the standards for Dietrich Bonhoeffer's own life," says Bethge. "It gave him a certainty of judgment and manner that cannot be acquired in a single generation" (*DB* 13).

Bonhoeffer was quite conscious of this heritage and valued it highly. While he was imprisoned, his niece Renate married his closest friend, Eberhard Bethge. When they had a baby, whom they named Dietrich,[10] Bonhoeffer wrote a baptismal message that reflects his desire to pass on the family spirit:

> The cosmopolitan culture of the old middle-class tradition represented by your mother's [i.e Renate, Dietrich's niece] home has created, in those who inherit it, a proud awareness of being called to high responsibility in public service, intellectual achievement and leadership, and a deep-rooted obligation to be guardians of a great historical heritage and intellectual tradition. This will endow you, even before you are aware of it, with a way of thinking and acting that you can never lose without being untrue to yourself (*DBWE* 8:384).

Dietrich's paternal grandmother, Julie Tafel Bonhoeffer, was from a family of very progressive thinkers and activists. She was a woman of strong character and strong backbone. When the Nazis declared April 1, 1933, a day for all Germans to boycott Jewish businesses, ninety-one-year-old Julie simply and fearlessly walked past the Storm Troopers to shop in her favorite store, which happened to be Jewish (*DB* 11).

Dietrich was about six years old when he gave a hint of the kind of person he was to become. Spotting a dragonfly, he whispered to his mother, "Look! There is a creature over the water! But don't be afraid, I will protect you."[11] Noble and protective, this little boy would someday gain such empathy for the needy and downtrodden that he would expand his compassion to embrace all the world.

In the end, working to protect all the world from a truly evil creature, he paid with his life.

Youth And Education

While we may safely assume that the faith of Dietrich Bonhoeffer was significantly influenced by the living examples of his mother and his governess, we cannot find equally good indicators about how he came to choose a career in theology. Perhaps he thought it to be a good blending of the academic values he had learned from his father and the faith he had learned from his mother. We will likely never know because he kept his inner motivations and even most of his feelings to himself, much as did his father.

What we do know is, first, his decision was firm by age fourteen, when he declared his intention to his family and, second, it would be years before he would fully comprehend the connection between faith and theology. His faith would have made theology an intriguing subject, but his intellectual environment must have made it almost unthinkable that theology could be anything more than a set of ideas to be studied like any other academic discipline. He did not yet know that all true theology is *"church* dogmatics,"[12] that ministry precedes theology as surely as love precedes understanding. Nor was he yet convinced that only believers can do theology rightly because theology is a field which can only be known from the inside out.[13]

The intellectual life came naturally to Bonhoeffer. He was extremely bright and serious, saw careful scholarship exemplified in his father and older brothers, and was raised with world-class scholars as family friends and neighbors. By age thirteen he was already devouring the classics in the humanities.[14] By the time he entered the university he was apparently far better educated than most college graduates in America even today.[15]

Just as natural for Dietrich was the spiritual life he had seen embodied in his mother and governess. We have an especially poignant reminder of that in Dietrich's Bible, in which his mother had inscribed,

> 2 Cor. 3:6—The letter kills, but the Spirit gives life.
> Rom. 13—He who loves his neighbor has fulfilled the law.

The internalizing of the first quotation would protect him from ever becoming a fundamentalist. The second—as he came to a mature understanding of its implications—would protect him from allowing theology to become an abstract discipline of the mind.

These inscribed words would have been deeply important to Dietrich, not only because they were in the hand of his beloved mother but because the Bible, which she gave him when he was confirmed, had belonged to his older brother, Walter. The references in his mother's hand were, in fact, written for Walter, who was killed in the First World War. The Bonhoeffer parents grieved deeply and seemed to take years to recover, so it is certain that none of the younger children ever forgot the heartache of their parents. It is equally certain that Dietrich never forgot that his Bible was Walter's.

Bonhoeffer first entered the university at Tübingen in 1923, though he stayed for only two semesters. Tübingen was something of a family tradition, though Dietrich was really more interested in the world-renowned faculty at Berlin. Before beginning at Berlin, he and his brother Klaus fulfilled another family tradition: a long stay in Rome.

With his knowledge of history and the family background in art, Dietrich was well prepared to enjoy the richness of this historic city. To his surprise, what caught his attention even more than the history was the freshness of faith he saw in the Catholic people of Rome. He was accustomed to the church being little more than a collection of ancient buildings and stale traditions, but in Rome he found himself captivated by the incredible range and beauty of the choirs and by the throngs of truly devout worshipers. He was learning how important the empirical church can be in the life of the believer.

Easter week found him in one worship service after another, most commonly at St. Peter's but often in others. On the evening of Palm Sunday he attended Mass at St. Peter's, sat for a time in the Colosseum, then walked to the Trinità dei Monti, at the head of the famous Spanish Steps, to enjoy the Vespers service. In his diary he wrote that this experience was:

almost indescribable. Around 6 o'clock approximately 40 young girls who wanted to become nuns entered in a solemn procession wearing nun's habits with blue or green sashes. The organ began to play. With unbelievable simplicity, grace, and great seriousness they sang Evensong while a priest officiated at the altar. [As they sang] every trace of routine was missing. The ritual was truly no longer merely ritual. Instead, it was worship in the true sense. . . . The day had been magnificent. It was the first day on which something of the reality of Catholicism began to dawn on me—nothing romantic, etc.—but I think I'm beginning to understand the concept of "church" (*DBWE* 9:88).

Dietrich was never attracted to the Catholic Church as an institution or to Catholic theology, probably because it was all too "religious" for him, yet he was so deeply touched by the experiences in Rome that the church was never again far from the center of his theology. His doctoral dissertation, completed just three years after the trip to Rome, was devoted to the nature of the church.

Returning from Rome, he enrolled in the university at Berlin, wanting to study with the foremost theological scholars in the world. He was a brilliant student who earned the respect of all his professors even though they were a bit baffled by his nonconformity to their liberal ways of thinking. Of particular interest for evangelicals is a paper he wrote for Professor Seeburg, a paper which brought him a merely passing grade, the lowest of his academic career. The essay is a critical examination of then current academic studies of the Scriptures. Still only 19 years old but already confident, he could challenge the great scholars. Bonhoeffer defended an approach to the Bible which he had learned from his mother and which stayed with him all his life. The paper was entitled "The Historical and Pneumatological Interpretations of Scripture."

Regarding the form of the Bible, with this [critical] approach the concept of the canon disintegrates and becomes meaningless. Textual and literary criticism are applied to the Bible. The sources are distinguished, and the methods of the history of religions and form criticism fragment the larger and even the remaining short textual units into little pieces. After this total disintegration of the texts, historical criticism leaves the field of battle. Debris and fragments are left behind. Its work is apparently finished. (*DBWE* 9:286).

Bonhoeffer is not rejecting critical scholarship. Rather, he is saying such scholarship does not go far enough. To use a more recent term, critical scholarship deconstructed the text without ever moving to a reconstruction appropriate to the Bible's actual value as the living Word of God.[16]

The more complete way of studying Scripture moves through the analytic stage to what Bonhoeffer calls "pneumatological" interpretation. By that he means gaining an understanding of the text by listening for the voice of the Holy Spirit in the passage. This sounds very much like the way he would have learned Bible study from his mother. Remember, she had written in the Bible given to Dietrich at his confirmation a quotation from 2 Corinthians 3:6, "The letter kills, but the Spirit gives life."

In his preface to the first edition of his great commentary on Romans, Barth said that ". . . my whole energy of interpreting has been expended in an endeavour to see through and beyond history into the spirit of the Bible, which is the Eternal Spirit."[17] That describes well just what Bonhoeffer wanted to do in his biblical studies—to see into or to hear the very Spirit of God.

One of the paper's great problems, from an academic perspective, is that "listening for the voice of the Spirit" is not a task that can be brought easily under intellectual discipline and control. As we often hear, one can make all sorts of claims about what the Spirit says. Such claims, many of which are patently ridiculous, cannot be easily disproved by rational means. One who truly listens for the Spirit of God must be a person of great integrity and be a person who takes part in communal discernment.

I still chuckle when I remember being asked to speak at a conference sponsored by a charismatic youth ministry. The afternoon opened with a guitar player leading us in singing choruses requested by any of us. Finishing one song and waiting for another request, the guitar player strummed for a minute or so, then blurted out the name of a popular song, saying, "That's a good one to get the Spirit moving." I tried without success to imagine the Holy Spirit of God lounging about, waiting for just the right song to be sung. Like the song leader, we are always in danger of confusing our own spirit with God's.

One of my favorite professors, Edward John Carnell, spoke of a "third method of knowing." We know by acquaintance and we know by inference. The deepest truths, however, can only be known by moral uprightness, moral self-acceptance.[18] "Truth by integrity" certainly describes what Bonhoeffer was seeking. Revelation must be met with integrity or it will be twisted.

We hear in Bonhoeffer's paper on biblical interpretation a hint of what will later become one of the central ideas in his understanding of the Christian life: We are to live not by rules or traditions but by the will of God. How is the will of God to be known? Though he does not develop the idea, the implication is that we know the will of God by listening to the Spirit of Jesus Christ, just as we know the Bible by listening to that same Spirit.

Early Career

Bonhoeffer earned his doctorate in 1927, at the age of 21, with a dissertation entitled *Sanctorum Communio (Communion of Saints)*. It was an exploration of the nature of the church, which he defined not as an institution or a hierarchy of authorities but as the *koinonia*, the fellowship, the community of believers. To conceive of the church in this way entails a clear understanding of the concept of person, the "building block" of the church. This, says Clifford Green, is the "central theological category" of the dissertation.[19] Such ideas, of course, could hardly be fit into any of the usual academic categories, but Dietrich's work was so intelligently presented that the faculty could not have considered withholding his degree.

The striking thing about this dissertation was not just that he saw the church in social rather than institutional terms but that he saw the church as the revelation of God. We know God as we come to know our brothers and sisters in Christ, who reveals himself in and through our communion together. He used a very strong phrase to make his point, speaking of "Christ existing as church community."[20] To see Jesus Christ, to see the self-revelation of God in Jesus Christ, we must look to the church.

We are taken aback by this idea. We are so aware of short-comings in ourselves and in our churches that we are often more inclined to apologize for them than to commend them as those communities in which God makes himself known.

Bonhoeffer will never leave behind this conviction, though in later years he will spell out two extensions of his understanding of the church. First, he will come to see personal confession as essential in the life of a fellowship. This means, as he will show in the book *Life Together*, that the church is grounded in the reality of human existence, not in some unrealistic ideals about how good we might be. Second, as he thinks matters through again while in prison during the war, he realizes that Jesus Christ lives *for others* and, therefore, the church in which Christ is revealed must itself be a church for others.

In February of 1928, Bonhoeffer took a one-year position—something of an internship—in a German congregation in Barcelona. He was still planning on being ordained but would not be eligible until he reached age 25, nor was he yet sure whether to pursue a life of academics or ministry. In his new assignment he assisted a somewhat disinterested pastor who allowed him a great deal of freedom but cautioned him not to be too ambitious. The pastor seems not to have wanted the congregation's expectations to be raised, thus leaving him to look bad after Bonhoeffer's departure.

In Barcelona, Bonhoeffer preached fairly often. His first sermon was on the text, "But if it is by grace, it is no longer on the basis of works, otherwise grace would no longer be grace" (Romans 11:6; *DBWE* 10:480). He thus began with an exposition of the classic Lutheran conviction of "justification by grace alone." Choosing such a beginning point, always to be seen in conjunction with the equally fundamental "justification by faith," Dietrich in effect was giving notice of the starting point for his own theological journey. Though the subject of justification is not always prominent in his later writings, that is only because of the intense pressure of the times, forcing him quickly to develop his understanding far beyond the basics. In writing the letters that were smuggled out of prison to his friend Bethge, Bonhoeffer assumes he and Bethge share a common foundation in justification by faith. Little in his writing makes sense apart from this grounding.

A further point of interest in this sermon is something which clearly is a prelude to the religionless Christianity of which he later writes: "One question forces itself upon us now. Is it all over for our religion and our morality, if none of that can lead us to God and if

God's paths are indeed different from our paths?" He assures his listeners that religion and morality will not disappear but warns that, "Religion and morality pose the most serious threat to knowledge of divine grace, for they bear the germ of wanting to find one's own way to God, to make oneself master over God. . ." (*DBWE* 10:483).

Bonhoeffer also gave several lectures while in Barcelona, perhaps partly to fulfill his own need for careful academic thought and partly to raise the level of theological understanding in the congregation. One was given on December 11, 1928, when he was all of twenty-two years old. The lecture is entitled "Jesus Christ and the Essence of Christianity." The opening lines are a strong challenge to us, as they certainly must have been to the Germans in Barcelona.

> We all know that, for all practical purposes, Christ has been eliminated from our lives. Although we still build his temple, we live in our own houses. Christ, instead of being the center of our lives, has become a thing of the church, or of the religiosity of a group of people. To the nineteenth and twentieth century mind, religion plays the part of the so-called parlor into which one doesn't mind withdrawing for a couple of hours, but from which one then immediately returns to one's place of work.
>
> However, one thing is clear, namely, that we understand Christ only if we commit to him in an abrupt either-or, He was not nailed to the cross as an ornamentation or decoration for our lives. If we want to have him, we must recognize that he makes crucial claims on our entire lives.
>
> The religion of Christ is not the tidbit after the bread; it is the bread itself or it is nothing. Those who would call themselves Christians should understand and acknowledge at least that much (*DBWE* 10:342).

Bonhoeffer would have had little patience with such cliches as when we speak of wanting God "to be a part of my life," as if the Creator of the universe were worthy of just one segment of our attention. We also speak of a devotional time as "spending a little time with God," as if all the other hours of the day were not spent with God. Sometimes we say that Jesus Christ is number one on our list of priorities, as if he himself were not the entire list. Bonhoeffer recognized what an abomination it is to relegate God to some part of our lives, our hearts, our schedules. Jesus Christ is not to be first on our list—Jesus is the list!

So we see that as early as age twenty-two Bonhoeffer understands that Jesus Christ is the sole, rightful, and all-encompassing center and circumference of a person's life. Bonhoeffer will understand this more deeply in his future years but he will never stray from his conviction that all of life is to be devoted to Christ. In just a few years, he will be expanding these ideas in what was to become his most popular book, *Discipleship*.[21]

In his 1928 lecture, one line is especially startling: "Christianity conceals within itself a seed hostile to the church."[22] I like that! Over and over again, fresh movements of the Spirit of God have been "captured" by policymakers who want to preserve something good but end up with power and control but no fresh Spirit. The work of the Wesleys, for example, was a major transformative experience in the moral and spiritual life of eighteenth century England, but it resulted in a denomination called the *Method*ist Church. It was the methods that were preserved, not the Spirit. Eventually the "Holiness" revival and then the Pentecostal revival had to break out of the institutional restraints of Methodism. Real Christianity—the living Christ!—continually has to break through the encrustations of policies and traditions.

At this point, there are two trains of thought for Bonhoeffer. One is that we experience Christ in community. The other is that Christ is the center of life for each individual. Were one to ask the young Bonhoeffer how the two ideas relate to one another, he might have been a bit uncertain of his answer. The fusion of the individual and the community in Bonhoeffer's thought became clear in the next decade to come.

We recognize that Bonhoeffer's idea of choosing for or against Christ—but not trying to find some middle ground, some partial commitment—is a reflection of the words of Christ as quoted in Revelation:

> I know your works; you are neither cold nor hot. I wish that you were either cold or hot. So, because you are lukewarm, and neither cold nor hot, I am about to spit you out of my mouth (Revelation 3:15-16).

We also hear a foretaste of C. S. Lewis, who would say in a 1943 BBC radio broadcast:

> You can shut [Jesus] up for a fool, you can spit at Him and kill Him as a demon; or you can fall at His feet and call Him Lord and God. But let us not come with any patronising nonsense about His being a great human teacher. He has not left that open to us.[23]

There is a certain absoluteness, a firm concreteness about Jesus Christ that is lost when we reduce him to just one aspect of his person, such as some doctrine or another about who he is. Later, in an essay entitled "Concerning the Christian Idea of God," apparently written as a class paper at Union Seminary in 1931 but shortly thereafter published in *The Journal of Religion* 12 (1932), Bonhoeffer would say:

> Personality as reality is beyond idea. . . . Thus Christ becomes not the teacher of mankind, the example of religious and moral life for all time, but the personal revelation, the personal presence of God in the world (*DBWE* 10:456).

A few weeks later, shortly before his departure from Barcelona, Bonhoeffer delivered another lecture just as radical and perhaps even more surprising than the earlier one: "Basic Questions of a Christian Ethic" (*DBWE* 9:359ff), in which he advances ideas every bit as shocking as those found in his later writings.

"Ethics," he says, "is a matter of blood and a matter of history. . . . It is a child of the earth. . . ." That is to say, ethics is shaped by culture and context. The search for a timeless "Christian" ethic is fruitless because "there are not and cannot be Christian norms and principles of a moral nature." Christianity, simply put, "is basically amoral" (*DBWE* 10:360).

He had already announced this theme, without development, in the earlier lecture on *The Essence of Christianity*:

> Religion and morality can become the most dangerous enemy of God's coming to human beings, the most dangerous enemy of the Christian message of good news. Thus the Christian message is basically amoral and irreligious, paradoxical as that may sound (*DBWE* 10:353f).

Why can there not be timeless Christian norms? Because rules and regulations, norms and principles are a kind of intermediary between us and Christ, letting us assume that if we follow the rules we must be pleasing to Christ. More seriously, when we abide by principles, we remain in control of our own lives because we are the ones doing the choosing of what to do in this situation or that.[24]

> Christianity speaks of the exclusive path from God to human beings from within God's own compassionate love toward the unholy, the sinful, while ethics speaks of the path from human beings to God. . . . In other words, the Christian message speaks of grace while ethics speaks of righteousness (*DBWE* 10:363).

Furthermore, Bonhoeffer argues:

> The Christian message stands beyond good and evil,[25] and this is how it must be; for if God's grace is made dependent on human beings according to the categories of good and evil, this would constitute a human claim on God. This, however, would challenge the power and honor due exclusively to God (*DBWE* 10:363).

And again, "There are no moral principles enabling Christians, as it were, to make themselves moral" (*DBWE* 10:365). The key phrase here is "to make themselves" into moral persons. Goodness and cleanness are gifts from God, not achievements of the human will.

Our concern, he argues, is not with the question of what is good but what is godly. More specifically, he is calling us to obey God directly, not indirectly through principles and rules.[26] That requires of us a level of maturity that can only come from long experience in walking with God.

With such an understanding of ethics in his mind at such an early age, Bonhoeffer was not in danger—as are we evangelicals—of becoming like the Pharisees in Jesus' day, wanting to please God by obeying his rules as literally as possible. What the Pharisees did not envision was the possibility of *knowing* God directly. They had little or no sense of a more living relationship, beyond mere obedience.

Bonhoeffer notes that,

> One particularly profound feature of the old story of the fall is that it was caused by eating from the tree of the knowledge of good and evil. That primal—let us say, childlike—community between human beings and God stands beyond this knowledge of good and evil; it knows

only one thing: God's limitless love for human beings (*DBWE* 10:363).

To help us understand what Bonhoeffer is saying, let us imagine that some fellow is angry at his neighbor and wants to kill him. To do so would be bad. He remembers that the Ten Commandments say we are not to murder, so he refrains. That is good—in a sense. What God is seeking in us, however, is not the goodness that comes from a negative ethic—"Thou shalt not . . ."—but something quite beyond this. God would be most pleased and most honored if the angry fellow would love his neighbor, not merely refrain from killing him.

That we evangelicals are made uncomfortable with Bonhoeffer's "amoral Christianity" shows how little we have thought about Jesus' teaching that love is the great commandment. It is far more comfortable to evade responsibility than to accept the challenge to love. In fact, Paul teaches that the whole law is summed up in the one word, love.

> Ethical decisions lead us into the most profound solitude, the solitude in which a person stands before the living God. Here no one can help us, no one can bear part of the responsibility; here God imposes a burden on us that we must bear alone. Only in the realization that we have been addressed by God, that God is making a claim on us, does our self awaken (*DBWE* 10:367).

We are responsible *for* ourselves but we are responsible *to* God. That is Bonhoeffer's idea of a mature Christian life. In the last century or more in America, there has been a tendency for some Christians to celebrate the idea that we are responsible for ourselves, which sounds like a great freedom. Other Christians, evangelicals among them, have centered their thinking on the idea that we are responsible to God, making the slip into legalism almost inevitable. Bonhoeffer never lost the connection between being responsible *to* God *for* ourselves.

Much later in his life, in the *Letters and Papers*, Bonhoeffer will express this idea even more dramatically—too dramatically for some—in saying, "Before God, and with God, we live without God."[27] We'll wait until later to explore that idea.

One final note from this lecture is important because of how Bonhoeffer would come to live it out in ways he could not have imagined when he first spoke these words. "If for a single dangerous moment I do not act," he said, "then I am doing nothing other than surrendering my neighbors" (*DBWE* 10:3731). Clearly the love for one's neighbor is of fundamental importance for Bonhoeffer as he envisions the God-responsive life. From his family life, he had already learned, of course, that his neighbors included the Jews.

In the background of these radical ideas are two of Bonhoeffer's most fundamental convictions. First, we are always and only to be Christ-centered in our lives, our thoughts, our decisions. Second, we are to mature beyond the child's stage of needing to be told what to do, needing someone else to take responsibility for our lives. We will find these twin affirmations forming the ground for nearly all that Bonhoeffer is to say from this point on.

No one who reads with care these two lectures by the very young Bonhoeffer can claim to be surprised by the radical language of his two most mature works, *Ethics* and *Letters and Papers*. An amazing thing about him is not where his theological thinking led him but that he seems to have been a creatively and radically faithful and insightful Christian from very early on.

Returning to Berlin in early 1929 Bonhoeffer took a position at the university as a teaching assistant while working on a second dissertation. The first dissertation had earned him a doctorate, but in order to be qualified to teach in a German university a second dissertation, the "habilitation thesis," is required. Like the first, this dissertation was also published. The title is *Act and Being* (*DBWE* 2), a topic much debated in German philosophical circles at that time.

Bonhoeffer's concern is not philosophy but theology, so the question is framed a bit differently: Does the revealing of God occur in the deeds of God or somehow directly, being-to-being? Bonhoeffer seeks to show that Jesus Christ merges and transcends the alternatives.

Because *Act and Being* shows even greater sensitivity to academic concerns than did *The Communion of Saints*, it has had little reading over the decades. It is difficult, philosophical, and for most non-scholars, very dry. Bonhoeffer himself never referred to it again, yet it remains a foundational document of how he philosophically understood God's revelation. It is worth noting that, from this time on, Bonhoeffer wrote in a much more popular style without ever leaving behind his own level of academic excellence.

So we return to the question: Was Dietrich Bonhoeffer like a modern American evangelical? The answer remains no, decidedly no. Evangelicalism is an Anglo-American culture of answers and attitudes built around a particular set of core beliefs. To a great degree, we share the deepest core of our beliefs with Bonhoeffer, yet there are some themes common among evangelicals but missing in Bonhoeffer, such as a concern for private, personal salvation and a desire to take the Bible as it is, without a critical reading.

More importantly, Bonhoeffer sees, values, and explores implications of our core beliefs and thereby builds on the foundation a house very unlike that of evangelicalism. His concern for justice, which will show up later in our explorations, is a real enigma for us. We once were champions of justice but were humiliated by the Scopes Trial and Prohibition, so in a classic case of sour grapes we retreated and said we valued only the Gospel instead. Then the Moral Majority tried again to speak out in the pubic square but gave up, saying society is beyond hope.[28]

As I look back over the early years of Dietrich Bonhoeffer, asking what lessons we evangelicals can learn, what first comes to mind is the nurturing of faith he received from his mother. She would never have considered entrusting to the church the faith-development of her children. That was strictly the responsibility of parents, she believed.

In our day, especially in Great Britain and the United States, the task of inculcating the faith in the lives of our children has been relegated to Sunday school. We think that forty-five minutes of a weekly class, usually led by an untrained teacher, will suffice. That is such a grave error that my own inclination is to say Sunday school is one of the bigger mistakes in the history of the church.

The first Sunday school classes were a part of what we would now call "social justice." Sparked by newspaper editor Robert Raikes in Gloucester, the intent was to provide basic training in reading and writing, using the Bible as the textbook, for the vast majority of children in England who did not attend school, since no public schools yet existed. Raikes thought that such an education might help prevent some of the slum children from growing up into a life of crime. The movement became so popular so quickly that England took note. There were many calls for free, public education, though In fact it was not fully established until 1870.

As child labor laws began to free younger children from enforced labor, especially in the mines, and as other educational opportunities began to develop, the churches which had first sponsored Sunday schools as a form of community service, started incorporating the program into their regular Sunday schedule and calling it Christian Education. It was meant, of course, only to complement the faith education the children were receiving from their parents.

In our day, with parents often completely uninvolved in the Christian education of their children and just as often not even sharing their own faith experiences with their children, Sunday school carries nearly all the burden of faith development.

Having spent ten years in university campus ministry, I am convinced that our idea of Christian Education is of little value in the lives of our children. During those years on campus I met only a handful of students who were grounded in a thoughtful faith. No Sunday school can begin to compare with Paula Bonhoeffer telling her children Bible stories and leading them in hymns and prayer each evening. In this way, Dietrich was taught to think, to read, and to articulate from the very beginning.

Another observation from my days in campus ministry is that evangelical students are usually completely unprepared for the challenges to their faith they face on campus and in the classroom. For the most part, they have been taught a few ideas to believe but not how to evaluate those ideas biblically and critically and to articulate them in an intelligible way. They have been taught to reject all competing ideas without asking what we might learn from those who differ with us. In other words, most evangelical students come to the university with a very immature faith.

So in Dietrich Bonhoeffer we find an affirmation of our faith and yet a great challenge to grow beyond our beginnings, to measure up to the fullness of the stature of our Lord Jesus Christ.

Endnotes

1. We must note from the beginning that, in the older German context, young men were considered to be "youth" throughout their 20s.
2. *DBWE* 8:384.
3. "The Younger Generations's Altered View of the Concept of Führer," *DBWE* 12:266.
4. See the excellent discussion of responsibility as the heart of Christian vocation in Lori Brandt Hale's "Bonhoeffer's Christological Take on Vocation" in *Bonhoeffer: Christ and Culture* (Westmont, Illinois: InterVarsity Press, 2013).

5   Along with many others, I confess to just a bit of envy. How I wish we evangelicals could nurture families like Dietrich's!

6   Sabine Leibholz Bonhoeffer, *The Bonhoeffer's: Portrait of a Family*, English edition (New York: Covenant Publications, 1994): 5.

7   Established in the early eighteenth century in eastern Germany, the Herrnhut community was and is the center of the worldwide Moravian Brethren movement. Much like classic Lutheran Pietism, the Moravian Brethren have a deep respect for the Bible, a deep devotion to Jesus Christ, and an active commitment to serving people. Moravian Brethren began sending international missionaries long before other Protestant groups. In 1736, John Wesley was on a ship headed for America when he became acquainted with Brethren whose faith touched and affected him deeply.

8   *Portrait*: 6.

9   *Last Letters of Resistance*, 104. Dietrich's twin Sabine remembers this happening when they were about twelve years old, Bethge 2000, 38.

10 Dietrich Bethge is a cellist and founder of the chamber orchestra called London Octave. Among other matters, Bonhoeffer had written in the baptismal message: "Music, as your parents understand and practice it, will bring you back from confusion to your clearest and purest self and perceptions, and from cares and sorrows to the underlying note of joy."

11 E. Metaxas, *Bonhoeffer: Pastor, Martyr, Prophet, Spy.* (New York: Nelson Bros., 2011), 11.

12 Karl Barth's magnum opus is the multivolume *Church Dogmatics*. It was first titled *Christian Dogmatics*. Barth changed the name in the second edition because he had realized that theology is best done not in the academy but in the living faith of the people of God.

13 Cf. his essay "The Christian Idea of God" (DBWE 10:454).

14 *Last Letters*, 97.

15 When studying in America, Bonhoeffer found discussions with American seminarians, all college graduates, to be like talking with twelfth graders. *Portrait*, 63.

16 Liberal theology in the broader sense, however, does take a bit of a beating later, in Bonhoeffer' lectures on christology, delivered in the summer of 1933. He says there that liberal theology has destroyed itself by failing to establish its own presupposition, that Jesus was not Christ but only became Christ in the eyes of the faithful. See *DBWE* 12:328.

17 Karl Barth, *The Epistle to the Romans*, translated by Edwyn C. Hoskyns, Sixth Edition (Oxford: Oxford University Press 1968), 1.

18 Edward John Carnell, *Christian Commitment* (London: MacMillan, 1957).

19 Clifford Green, Introduction to *Ethics*, *DBWE* 6:3. Green calls this a "theology of sociality" and notes that it "proved to be fundamental for all of Bonhoeffer's writings, including *Ethics*."

20 Oddly enough, the phrase comes from Hegel, who could never have guessed the richness that Bonhoeffer found in those words (*DB* 83).

21 Early English editions were entitled *The Cost of Discipleship*.

22 "Jesus Christ As the Essence of Christianity," *DBWE* 10:354.

23 C. S. Lewis, *Mere Christianity*. There are many editions available. These are the concluding lines of the third chapter of the section called "What Christians Believe."

24 See another explication of this idea in the section called "Who Stands Firm?" in Bonhoeffer's much later essay, "After Ten Years," *DBWE* 8:38f.

25 This, of course, is a phrase made famous by Friedrich Nietzsche, one of whose books is entitled *Beyond Good and Evil*. Nietzsche called for an *Übermensch*, one who would rise above all human convention and be a law unto himself. It was an idea which Hitler liked to use for himself. Bonhoeffer calls us to move beyond good and evil not to super-arrogance, to hubris, but to responsiveness to our living Lord.

26 We cannot miss here the similarity to Bonhoeffer's ideas about biblical interpretation, as we saw in his student essay on "The Historical and the Pneumatological Interpretation of Scripture," in which he saw the interpretation of the Bible by historical and critical studies to be insufficient. What is necessary in biblical understanding, he was already convinced at that young age, was that we be ever listening for and to the Spirit of God.

27 Letter of 16 July 1944, *DBWE* 8:479.

28 Noted in a 1992 lecture by Ed Dobson, Falwell's partner in the Moral Majority, in a lecture at Concordia College, Moorhead, Minnesota.

CHAPTER TWO

Time of Great Change

"We no longer read the Bible seriously; we no longer read it against ourselves, but for ourselves."[1]

New York

Bonhoeffer spent the 1930-1931 school year at Union Seminary in New York, recipient of a Sloan Fellowship for international students. It was an almost comical year, with Bonhoeffer fully qualified to be a professor himself and the American graduate students seeming to him more like twelfth-grade boys.[2] In a way, he was simply passing time until he became 25, the age at which he would be eligible for ordination in the church and for an academic appointment.

Yet, in some ways this was the most important year of his life and certainly had a profound influence on his future.[3] It was not the classroom experience that mattered most, since he found the American classroom and American students to be greatly disappointing. He found no rigorous study and little substantial theological discipline. Instead, the Americans seemed merely to confuse ethics with theology.[4]

We must be careful here not to assume that because Bonhoeffer was rejecting liberalism, in a sense, that he must have been more like a modern evangelical since he was devoted to Jesus and Bible.[5] Bonhoeffer's dissatisfaction was caused by the American's lack of theological foundations for their ethical views, while the Fundamentalists simply didn't warrant his attention. He did not reject liberalism so much as American education and scholarship. He also did not embrace evangelicalism since it didn't even exist in any form similar to what is called evangelicalism in America today. He was a friendly critic from within liberalism.

The greater influence on Bonhoeffer came outside the classroom in friendships with students and in his discovery of the American Black churches.[6] The students with whom he was closest were Paul Lehmann, a second-generation German-American, Erwin Sutz from Switzerland, Jean Lasserre from France, and Frank Fisher, a black American. These were friends with whom he could share deep and substantial conversation, who contributed to each other's learning and growing, who gave each other new insights into the Lord and the human heart.

Do we have such friends today? Are we such a friend for others?

Lehmann served as something of a big brother for Bonhoeffer in America, helping him find his way around New York streets and American customs. Sutz became Bonhoeffer's point of connection with the great Swiss theologian Karl Barth, whom Bonhoeffer admired but had not met. Lasserre opened to Dietrich a whole new world of what we today might call spiritual formation, particularly in his understanding of the Sermon on the Mount as a very personal guide to a lifestyle of following Jesus. Bonhoeffer's later book *Discipleship*, based in large part on the Sermon on the Mount, grew out of his friendship with Lasserre.

Frank Fisher opened to Bonhoeffer a very different world indeed: the black churches of Harlem. A highly reserved German gentleman with a powerful intellect, Bonhoeffer found himself reveling in the highly expressive worship services of these black Americans. They were open, emotional, deeply engaged and engaging, and centered on a living Jesus on whom they were happily dependent. Beyond the walls of the church, they took care of one another as a normal part of being a community.

Having been dissatisfied with the churches he had been visiting, including the towering Riverside Church where the famous Harry Emerson Fosdick was preaching,[7] Bonhoeffer began attending Abyssinian Baptist Church nearly every Sunday, hearing the preaching of Adam Clayton Powell Sr. He did not remain a cool outsider but got to know and be known by the people. He was invited to teach Sunday school, which gave him great pleasure, and to visit in people's homes.

Reflecting on Powell's preaching, Bonhoeffer later wrote, "I heard the Gospel preached in the Negro churches. . . . Here one really could still hear someone talk in a Christian sense about sin and grace and the love of God and ultimate hope. . . ."⁸ One fellow student commented that Bonhoeffer returned from Abyssinian one day and with great and uncharacteristic excitement said it was the only time he had experienced true religion in the United States, and was convinced that it was only among blacks who were oppressed that there could be any real religion in this country (*DBWE* 10:31).

If *Discipleship* is the fruit of Bonhoeffer's friendship with Lasserre, then these lines from *After Ten Years*, written in December of 1942, speak of deep lessons learned from Fisher and the Black Baptists:

> It remains an experience of incomparable value that we have for once learned to see the great events of world history from below, from the perspective of the outcasts, the suspects, the maltreated, the powerless, the oppressed and reviled, in short from the perspective of the suffering. . . . [P]ersonal suffering is a more useful key, a more fruitful principle than personal happiness for exploring the meaning of the world in contemplation and action.⁹

It is not that Fisher and Harlem first awakened in Dietrich this focus on the powerless in society. While in Spain in 1928-29, he had been a careful observer of the lives of ordinary people, those quite unlike the privileged and intellectual elite of his German experience. Like Buddha coming out from behind the walls of the palace and seeing human suffering for the first time, Bonhoeffer in Spain was deeply moved by what he saw on the streets of Barcelona.

Even before reaching Spain he had begun to see life "from below." Traveling from Germany to Barcelona, he stopped in Paris and, among other visits, attended a Mass at the Sacré-Coeur Basilica. He wrote in response:

> The people in the church were almost all from Montmartre, prostitutes and their men went to the Mass and submitted to all the ceremonies . . . one saw . . . how close, through their fate and guilt, these heavily burdened people stood to the essence of the Gospel. I've believed for a long time that Tauentzienstrasse in Berlin would be an extremely fruitful field for church work. It is much easier for me to imagine a praying murderer or prostitute than a vain person. Nothing goes more against prayer than vanity (*DBWE* 10:159).¹⁰

As I read these words, my mind wanders back over the innumerable advertisements that crossed my desk as a pastor. Often, I would see that some conference or another was to be led by Pastor What's-his-name, whose congregation grew from fifty to 5,000 in just five years. American evangelicals have learned from the world to measure the value of pastoral ministry by the numbers, by "success" in attracting people and raising funds. In the minds of some, power and ambition seem to be apt traits for those claiming to be servants of Christ. The very signs of "good" ministry in these success-oriented contexts make it especially difficult to "see the great events of world history from below, from the perspective of the outcasts."

Compounding the problem for evangelicals is a fad that marked the 1980s and 1990s: Pastors were being taught that they should learn from secular businessmen how to be successful CEOs. A friend, knowing my particular interest in the Gospel of Mark, gave me a book by an National Football League team executive. It was a series of lessons on leadership, purportedly drawn from the work and teaching of Jesus as revealed in Mark. Very few of the "lessons" had even a slight connection to the text, and not one of them took into account Mark's purpose in writing. It was just another gee-pastor-here's-how-to-be-an-executive-like-me book, thinly disguised as biblical. Evangelical pastors, in whom great ambitions were being inspired, bought such books in great numbers.[11]

Berlin

Again Bonhoeffer returned to Berlin in the summer of 1931 and by November had embarked on his double career as professor and pastor. He began his academic career as an unpaid lecturer. Until receiving faculty appointments, young scholars were permitted to give lectures with the students donating whatever they liked to the lecturer. He remained in this position for two years, during which Adolf Hitler rose to power.

During those two years he offered both lectures and seminars. He lectured on twentieth century theology, the nature of the church, "Creation and Fall" in Genesis, and christology. His seminars included Philosophy and Protestant Theology, Christian Ethics, and Theological Anthropology.

Two of his classes are of particular interest for evangelicals, and the lectures from both of them became books published in the mid-

1930s in Germany. Neither attracted much attention at the time but since then—starting outside Germany—have received a wide reading. The first was his class on the early chapters of Genesis, published as *Creation and Fall* (*DBWE* 3). The second was his class on christology, published in an earlier English edition as *Christ the Center* and now included in his collected works simply as "Lectures on Christology" (*DBWE* 12:299).

Creation and Fall. *Creation and Fall* shows a certain kinship with the thinking of Karl Barth in that it is a "theological exposition," that is, something like what evangelicals call biblical theology, a study of the theology of the biblical books and writers. (Systematic or dogmatic theology has traditionally been regarded as a near-cousin to philosophy.) This was, as John de Gruchy notes, his "first attempt to do theology in direct dialogue with the Bible."[12] Unlike evangelical biblical theology, however, Bonhoeffer allows his creative instincts to explore with great care the implications of the text. "Theological exposition" occupies what we may call a certain middle ground between biblical and systematic theology.

Though it may seem unremarkable now, in fact it was quite courageous of Bonhoeffer to choose Genesis 1—3 for his class. Not only was the biblical portrait of creation considered irrelevant in university circles but—more significantly—the Old Testament itself was being dismissed in the emerging German mindset as a mere Jewish book.

It was perhaps just as remarkable that Dietrich chose to hold a class on a small portion of Scripture. Why would one spend so much time on just three chapters of the Bible? John de Gruchy tells us that "His concern was to hear the word of God that had spoken in the beginning—and that was seeking even then to speak to 'Germany and the nations of the world'" (*DBWE* 3:5).

This becomes a fundamental theme in Bonhoeffer's thinking, that in and through Scripture we hear the living word of God. We are reminded that this is where he began, advocating what he called the "pneumatological" understanding of the Bible.

Seeing Scripture as a "love letter from God," as a living word, leaves Bonhoeffer free to entertain all sorts of critical doubts. Bonhoeffer wrote, for example:

> in this passage the biblical author is exposed as one whose knowledge is bound by all the limitations of the

author's own time. Heaven and the sea were in any event not formed in the way the author says, and there is no way we could escape having a very bad conscience if we let ourselves be tied to assertions of that kind. The theory of verbal inspiration will not do. The writer of the first chapter of Genesis sees things here in a very human way.[13]

Evangelicals, to the degree that we have been influenced by the Pietist dimension of our historical backgrounds, are in perfect accord with the idea that the biblical revelation is conditioned to a very large degree by the cultural context of the writer. Biblical revelation is God's very personal self-revelation, not a scientific treatise on ancient geology. We have also been influenced, however, by the Enlightenment and earlier by the Western recovery of classical Greek philosophers, Aristotle in particular. For example, in Calvinism in particular, a strongly rationalist element entered orthodox theology. Reading Calvinist authors today, we find the words "logic" and "logical" among their verbal favorites.

I've just plucked from my bookshelf the book, *No Place for Sovereignty* by R. K. McGregor Wright,[14] and flipped through a couple of pages, finding this comment in one of his chapters challenging Arminianism:

> A reasoned argument requires correct presuppositions, a series of connected syllogisms or connected implications that do not violate the laws of logic, and at least one conclusion that is warranted by the premises. To a rational mind, such a conclusion is the stuff of real progress in the search for truth.[15]

The search for truth must be done in strict adherence to the laws of logic, says McGregor. His presupposition, of course, is that truth is a propositional statement of some sort. And *that* betrays the weak point of his argument. Theology is treated as a study of ideas, not so much of God directly.

The value of logic, so important in exploring ideas, is absolutely limited to the quality of the presuppositions, ideas which cannot be derived logically. Logic tells you how to get from Idea A to Idea B in a reliable fashion, but it does not tell you whether Idea A is true itself. Nonetheless, Wright represents a substantial side of evangelicalism, thinking of theology in essentially Greek terms requiring Greek methods of interpretation.

The problem with considering logic to be the primary vehicle of truth is that the deepest truths in life are personal, not ideological and not materialistic. Personal revelation can only be received and understood in ways quite unlike the ways that ideas are comprehended.

A generation ago, psychologist B. F. Skinner argued that reality lies "beyond freedom and dignity."[16] Such "human" qualities, he said, are mere illusions. Tell that to the grieving young woman who has just received a telegram telling her that her husband has been killed in action. Would even Skinner be so hard-hearted as to tell her that her grief is a mere illusion?

A decade later Bonhoeffer will look back on this period in his life and say that, while his mind had not fundamentally changed over the years, there was a bit of a shift in the early 1930s when his thinking moved "from the phraseological to the real."[17] One way of expressing that idea would be to say that he shifted his attention from the doctrine of Christ to the reality of Christ, from ideas about Christ to the living person of Christ. Those who speak of "propositional revelation"[18] as the high point of theology have not made such a shift. They are still doctrine-centered.

Have the adherents of "propositional revelation" not heard Jesus say, "*I* am the truth"?

Evangelicalism, then, has a somewhat bifurcated view of Scripture. Our Pietist heritage makes Bonhoeffer's approach to the Bible seem quite familiar to us because our faith is so personal, but our particular form of Enlightenment rationalism[19] clashes with Bonhoeffer's appreciation of critical studies.

The careful reader will find a great deal of richness—and challenge!—in the Genesis lectures of this twenty-six-year-old junior professor. Let me suggest some of the ways in which Bonhoeffer points us in directions worthy of careful meditation.

First, his opening line is, "The place where the Bible begins is one where our own most impassioned waves of thinking break, are thrown back upon themselves, and lose their strength in spray and foam" (*DBWE* 3:25). That is, the story of creation marks the absolute limit to which our mind can reach backwards in time. We cannot ask—because we cannot imagine—what God was like or what God was "thinking" before creation. We cannot even guess at his motivation. We simply accept the Bible's plain fact: God created.

But there is a valuable lesson to be learned from this limitation: Since God has revealed nothing of why he created, we can grasp only that he created in absolute freedom. So far as we can know, God did not create for a reason, not for a goal; he simply created. If we want to find a way to word this theologically, we can only say that all creation is purely an act of grace. All creation exists by and because of God's sheer grace.

Second, the story of creation "is not to be thought of in temporal terms" (*DBWE* 3:32). There is little or nothing to be gained by thinking of Genesis 1—3 as revelation about some particular time at the beginning of cosmic and human history. Rather, the passage reveals a spiritual source, not an historical beginning. "It is *our* primeval history, truly our own, every individual person's beginning, destiny, guilt, and end" (*DBWE* 3:82). What I read in the story of the creation of human beings is *my* story. I'm reading my own spiritual biography.

Time and again in counseling—especially premarital counseling—I found myself sharing this story of our beginning, the fountain of the human story. Helping people know themselves includes helping them know their roots, not just their biological but particularly their spiritual roots. These chapters express beautifully the spiritual source from which our very beings flow.

How do we see this connection between our being and our spiritual source? In Chapter One humans are created in the image of God. That means we are made for creativity, community, and caretaking over all the earth. Each of these implies responsibility. We are responsible and accountable to our Lord for what we do with his earth and his people.

Genesis 2:4 begins a second telling of the story of creation and it is a very different story. Less orderly and poetic, it seems more like the actual story of our past. Human is formed of dust, of the ordinary elements we find listed on the nutrition charts on many of our foods. As a second step God breathed life into this human. This image emphasizes the split we all wrestle with. We are of the earth yet we breathe the breath of God.

As yet another step in this second telling of the story, the Lord says, "It is not good that the man should be alone; I will make him a helper as his partner." Some hear these words as an insult to women. I read them as proof that I'm in need of a great deal of help. Each gender receives an equally gentle humbling.

Adam and Eve, we are told, were both naked and not ashamed. This is extremely important for us. To be naked and ashamed is to be vulnerable, defenseless, unprotected. But if we are naked and have no need for shame, we are loved, accepted, free to be ourselves without fear of judgment.

Then, they eat the forbidden fruit. Immediately they realize they are liable to judgment and rejection, so they grab fig leaves to create a flimsy protection for the dignity they've already lost. In premarital counseling I would pause here and ask the couple to begin spelling out how they will recognize their own vulnerability and their own fig leaves.

We also try to learn how to recognize God when he comes to rescue us. The story is amazing. He comes not with fury and accusation but with a simple question, "Where are you?" What a gentle way to invite the humans to reveal themselves. That question still hangs in the air for us, though we usually ask it in slightly different forms. Who are you? Who am I? What am I here for?

One final observation. In Genesis 5, we are told that the now-flawed Adam and Eve bear children in their own image. We are to have inherited *imago dei* from our parents, as they did from theirs. But the image we receive is actually a mixture of good and bad, of godliness and of resistance to God.

Third, we learn from this, our story, that we are who we are together. "Let us make humankind in our image," says our Creator, speaking in the plural. Our identity lies not within us as individuals but within us in community, in relationship. We are who we are in relation to God our creator. Just as importantly, we are who we are in relation to one another.[20]

This does not mean that we lose ourselves in the community. Quite the opposite, Bonhoeffer argues. We do not simply blend into the community as a drop of water into the sea.[21] In fact, we bump into each other! Whether we are thinking of our relationship with God or with one another (if we can separate the two at all), we must be careful not to think of losing ourselves. If we simply disappear into some sort of community existence (as cults often inculcate) we actually lose the relationship because we lose the individual. The community is two or more persons existing together but not fused together.

Thus, our freedom lies neither in resisting the demands put on us by others nor in losing ourselves in one another. Rather, we—created for community and needing to be the persons we were created to be—are most free, most truly ourselves, when we are free *for* others.

There is a warning to be noted here. If we're thinking of spatial images, of literally bumping into one another, we'll miss Bonhoeffer's insight. *"The human being's limit is at the center of human existence*, not on the margin" (*DBWE* 3:86). That is, the point of contact which defines who we are is at the center of our being. If we fail to contact, to relate center-to-center, we remain isolated and lack relationship. The fruit is loneliness and a loss of our sense of selfhood.

Adam and Eve ceased to be the persons they were created to be (as defined by their relationship with God) when they chose not to complement God but to compete with him, to become the lords of their own lives and make their own decisions about right and wrong. Having rejected their relationship with God, they also rejected themselves. And they even had to grab fig leaves to protect themselves from mutual rejection.

Fourth, technology, that wonderful offshoot of science, is both a blessing and a curse. The progress of science is allowing us previously undreamed of advances in both knowledge and technology. However, they put us in grave danger of breaking a third dimension of our relational identity: our relationship to the earth. We are creatures of the earth, lumps of clay molded by God, with spiritual life breathed into our nostrils (in the delightful imagery of Genesis 2). Technology seeks to improve on nature and to free us of natural limitations. Each technological advance is a step away from nature and is thereby another step in the denial of our own reality and identity. Can we learn to be technologically advanced while remaining children of the earth? That has not yet been determined.

Some scientists in our day have become completely beguiled by their own achievements and think they have supplanted God. Stephen Hawking, for example, believed the entire beginnings of our universe could be explained through sheer science alone without any need of a "god-hypothesis." It seems, however, that—to choose but one example—people's faith is not weakened by the observation that the Milky Way is just the appearance of our particular galaxy viewed from the inside. Rather, faith is weakened in those increasingly numerous people who have never seen the Milky Way because they never in their lives have been far enough away from electric lights.

At dusk last evening, with my wife and one of our granddaughters, I stood gazing for a long time at the most beautiful double rainbow I've ever seen, made especially awesome by the most incredibly delicate bolts of lightning that seemed to be dancing between the arcs of color. I know how science explains a rainbow and I have no doubt there is a scientific explanation for the very odd little spears of lightening, but no science in the world could have stopped me from saying, "Thank you, Lord; that's awesome."

Christ the Center. Bonhoeffer's christology lectures in the summer of 1933,[22] were created and delivered in tumultuous times. Hitler had become chancellor in late January, declared martial law in February, had begun subsuming the university and the church in March, and had begun marginalizing the Jews in April.[23] In that month, Bonhoeffer wrote his famous essay "The Church and the Jewish Question," in response to the Aryan Acts which began the formal rejection of the Jews. Then, very shortly after the conclusion of the christology course, Bonhoeffer moved to London in despair over the feeble responses of the church to the Nazis.

Bonhoeffer lectured on christology with only glimpses of the chaotic context. This testifies to the great importance of the subject for Dietrich, not to his disinterest in what was happening in Germany. Joel Lawrence notes the significance of Christ for Bonhoeffer from this time forward:

> His christology lectures represent another evolution in Bonhoeffer's theology: a more sustained Christocentrism in which his earlier focus on the community is not eclipsed, but through which his view of the community is more sharply focused. Jesus Christ gains a more central position in Bonhoeffer's theology, and also in his own life. Christ becomes the unifying vision for Bonhoeffer that would carry him through to the end of his life.[24]

Bonhoeffer a few months earlier had begun his lectures on Genesis by saying that we humans can only be silent before the miracle of creation. Creation is simply so far beyond our grasp that we cannot even ask a question about it. We simply accept the fact and begin from there. Just so, he now begins his christology lectures with the same idea. "In proclaiming Christ, the church falls on its knees in silence before the inexpressible, the αρρητου ['things too sacred to tell']. To speak of Christ is to be silent, and to be silent about Christ is to speak" (*DBWE* 12:300).

Certainly there are times when we speak or sing lightly and joyfully of Jesus, who is a delight to our souls. There must also be balancing times, however, when we pause to behold and be stunned anew by the miracle of the Word become Flesh. In modern evangelicalism, we have come close to losing entirely this second dimension of our love for Christ. We treat the Gospel so lightly that we are like children who come to church each Sunday to play "pick up sticks" with the Gospel and the Scriptures, not realizing these are sticks of dynamite! Annie Dillard grabs our attention when she writes:

> The churches are children playing on the floor with their chemistry sets, mixing up a batch of TNT to kill a Sunday morning. It is madness to wear ladies' straw hats and velvet hats to church; we should all be wearing crash helmets. Ushers should issue life preservers and signal flares; they should lash us to our pews.[25]

In these two sets of Bonhoeffer's lectures, there are at least two points which will make evangelicals nervous, two sticks of TNT.

First, he notes that it is Jesus—not the Bible—who is properly known as the Word of God. "The Logos became flesh," he writes, "and therefore cannot be restricted to the realm of mere words." We might say that evangelicals agree that Jesus is the Word but, in practice, very rarely if ever do we think of Jesus when we use the phrase, "Word of God."

This is no mere matter of a slightly different emphasis. Under Calvinist influence, we tend to think of revelation as being God's teaching about doctrine. We remain personally distant from that revelation. The ideas are "out there," to be believed or not. If, however, we consistently think of God's revelation, God's *Word*, as Jesus Christ himself, we are forced to respond as persons. Biblical truth is, as Jesus taught, primarily personal and only secondarily ideological or, in Bonhoeffer's later term, phraseological. Buddha may have said, I teach you the truth. Confucius said it too. Jesus said something quite different: "I *am* the way and the truth and the life" (John 14:6).

One implication of this Christ-centered (and quite biblical) understanding of the nature of truth as personal is that truth emerges in relationships. "Truth happens only in community [or communion] between two persons" (*DBWE* 12:317).Truth, we might say, is relational; it is not an entity carried around in the pocket of the brightest people. This fits perfectly with Bonhoeffer's earlier idea that Christ exists as community, in the church.

Second, Bonhoeffer shows he has little use for any doctrine of verbal inspiration. This follows very naturally from the biblical idea that truth is personal, not propositional.

> We have to read this book of books with all our human resources, and even as we do so, we remain in the profane world. This is very difficult ground on which we stand. For it is difficult to preach about words that history cannot prove were actually spoken by Jesus. On the other hand, verbal inspiration means to deny the Christ who alone is present as the Risen One. Inspiration from the literal words is a poor surrogate for the resurrection (*DBWE* 12:331).

In many ears, these will sound like insults against the Bible. We need to remember, though, that our idea of propositional revelation comes more from Aristotle than from Scripture itself.[26] Bonhoeffer sees the danger of misplacing our faith from Jesus to the Bible: The Book can become an intermediary between us and the Lord.

Just as there is a danger in Roman Catholicism of trusting the Church instead of the Lord, there is a risk in evangelicalism of trusting the Bible instead of the Lord.

Bonhoeffer held the Bible in extremely high regard, studied it more diligently and intensely than all but the rarest evangelicals, and listened to it always as a love letter from God. But what he listened for was the living voice of the Spirit of God, not a mere record of what God said to someone a long time ago. In Scripture, even in its fragility, "God comes to meet us as the Risen One" (*DBWE* 12:331).

We cannot fail to learn something very substantial from this emphasis on the Logos become flesh (rather than becoming a doctrine). "Because the Logos became flesh," Bonhoeffer says, "we cannot ask what or how questions, only "Who are you?" (*DBWE* 12:303). Or, in language common among evangelicals, we cannot ask questions to help us know *about* Jesus when the important thing is to ask questions that help us simply to *know* him.

Bonhoeffer has asked the personal question "Who?" only to discover that the question gets turned back on us and we find ourselves being asked by God, "Who are you, that you ask this question?" (*DBWE* 12:305).

We are reminded of the remarkable conversation between God and Moses, remembered for us in Exodus 3. God tells Moses he is to go back to Egypt to lead the people out of slavery. Moses, probably struggling with a great sense of shock, asks God, "Who am I that I should go to Pharaoh. . .?" God's answer is not at all like what Moses was expecting: "I will be with you." It is not some personal, private, individual sense of identity that God gives Moses. It is instead a declaration of the relationship which makes Moses who he is.

Then Moses, sensing there is a question which must be asked concurrently with the first question, asks how to explain to the people just who is sending him. In effect, he is asking of this God who has remained silent for four centuries, "Who are you?" The answer is a refusal to define himself, to distinguish himself from other "gods." The Lord says simply, "I am who I am."

The two questions must always come together: Who are you and who am I? Asking just one—as our culture is trying hard to do as it explores issues of personal identity—is like trying to fly an airplane with just one wing. A death spiral is the inevitable result. Again, this is because we are who we are together, in community.[27]

A further dimension of Bonhoeffer's insistence that truth is essentially personal is his observation about how we know and are known.

> There is no access to the human person, other than the person's decision to reveal himself. I cannot get to another person unless that person reveals himself to me. This self-revelation of one person to another, however, in reality takes place in the church of Jesus Christ, in the event of the forgiveness of sins, when one presents oneself to another as a sinner, confesses oneself to be a sinner, and receives from the other forgiveness for one's sin (*DBWE* 12:309).

Truth, personal truth, is known by revelation. This is a conviction Bonhoeffer shared with Barth, that revelation—not mere scholarly examination—is the means of knowing God. This is not a rejection of scholarship, as the whole of Barth's and Bonhoeffer's work makes clear, but it does mean that at the center of their personal and professional lives there is a sense of humility, of having to receive truth as a gift. God entrusts himself to us but cannot be discovered and certainly cannot be controlled by us.

Bonhoeffer surprises us, if we've not followed his thought since the writing of *Sanctorum Communio*, by insisting that God's revelation of himself "takes place in the church of Jesus Christ." This is true both for God's self-revelation and also for our own. That's why Bonhoeffer specifies that self-revelation must be met with forgiveness. If we do not accept one another freely and fully, overcoming flaws and sins by grace, neither will we be accepting the Lord fully and freely. And, as Jesus put it in the Sermon on the Mount, if we do not forgive, we are not forgiven (Matthew 6:15).

Since Adam and Eve first grabbed fig leaves to hide their vulnerability from one another, we have feared being known. To be known is to risk being rejected. We carry within us the perpetual sense that we deserve to be rejected. It is the assurance of forgiveness that gives us the boldness to be open about who we feel ourselves to be.

Self-revelation on God's part is a moment of vulnerability for him, just as it is with us. Yes, of course God is infinitely superior to us but that hardly means he is insensitive toward us. If our love matters to him, as it surely does, then so does our rejection of him.

God's self-revelation, therefore, comes to those prepared to accept him. Those who are determined to reject him will never be shown the truth and will never know the heart of God.

One further implication of the idea that God is known only by revelation is that only those who know God are trustworthy theologians. If theology is the study of the personal God, then a merely objective, rationalistic theology is blinded to the very center of its own work. As Bonhoeffer says in a 1932 article "Concerning the Christian Idea of God":

> The basis of all theology is the fact of faith. Only in the act of faith as a direct act [is] God recognized as the reality which is beyond and outside of our thinking, of our whole existence. Theology, then, is the attempt to set forth what is already possessed in the act of faith (*DBWE* 10:454).

Moving on in Bonhoeffer's story, we see that, at the same time as these beginnings in the world of university teaching, Bonhoeffer continued to be engaged in the life of the church with a two-pronged commitment. He worked with local church groups and also was active in international ecumenical work. He was ordained in November of 1931, having at last reached the required age of 25, and was then required to spend another year as an assistant pastor. He was sent not to a church but to fill a new position as chaplain to the students at a technical college. He was not at all opposed to working with students, having initiated student ministries in Barcelona and taught Sunday School in New York, but in this new position he had little success.

He was also assigned to teach a confirmation class in Berlin, taking over from a man whose spirit had been broken by the harassment of the students. Dietrich began by leaning against a wall, silently waiting for them to become bored with their own noise. As the din diminished, he began to speak softly, telling stories from Harlem. The boys quieted quickly and were never again a discipline problem.

Bonhoeffer wrote to his Swiss friend Erwin Sutz about the experience, saying that ". . . what helped the most was that I simply told them stories from the Bible with great emphasis, particularly the eschatological passages" (*DB* 226).

It is not clear whether we should laugh or cry at the way the church leaders were treating their brilliant young pastor. Were they drastically underestimating his gifts? Were they simply fearful of his genius? Were they already leery of his political leanings?

He also was sent to a number of international ecumenical conferences, during which time he became a significant leader among the younger participants in these conferences. Germans at the time tended to be both proud of their Germanic heritage and surprisingly insular, disdaining significant contact outside Germany. So even in this assignment, Bonhoeffer was not being entrusted with a valued responsibility.

Nonetheless, Bonhoeffer was gaining international respect and was frequently a speaker at ecumenical gatherings. At a youth conference in Gland, Switzerland in August of 1932, he spoke words which showed that the influence of Jean Laserre and the Sermon on the Mount was still stirring in him.

> Has it not become terribly clear, again and again, in all that we have discussed with one another here, that we

are no longer obedient to the Bible? We are more fond of our own thoughts than of the thoughts of the Bible. We no longer read the Bible seriously, we no longer read it against ourselves, but for ourselves (*DBWE* 11:377f).

These words are a strong challenge to—if not condemnation of—contemporary evangelicalism. We read the Bible and preach the Bible, if at all, strictly for what we can "get out of it," forgetting that the Bible is not meant to be simply a handbook for happy living. It is the revelation of the character, ways, promises, and expectations of God. We are not being invited to step up to the biblical buffet line and choose whatever tidbits happen to suit us. Rather, our task is to accept the challenge of Scripture, conforming our lives to the character of God as revealed in Jesus Christ through the Bible.

George Barna, a popular evangelical writer in the 1990s, serves as an example of how far the Bible has fallen in evangelical eyes. In his most popular book, *User Friendly Churches*, Barna observes:

Pastors of the user friendly churches tended to draw examples from the Bible of how Jesus utilized this [perceived-need] approach in His ministry. The common approach was for Him to begin to build a relationship by focusing on the needs of the other person, addressing those needs with tangible assistance, then sharing with them the larger, more enduring principles that would be of the greatest help in the long-run. The significance of Christ's strategy is underscored by the fact that disciples such as Peter and Paul relied on the very same approach.[28]

We see here the heart of the problem which causes this abuse. Notice that Barna is commending the pastors for drawing examples from the Bible to support their opinions. That is precisely the problem! Scripture has become a source of illustrations to exemplify lessons learned elsewhere. The Bible has been reduced to a mere collection of spiritual clip art! When the Bible is used only to illustrate the pastor's point, it is chained and caged, kept from its rightful prophetic role of speaking "against" us, examining us to see if we are living up to its message.

Much preaching today, especially in the mega-churches and the television churches, is geared exclusively toward teaching people how to be happy by getting all they can from God. One of the grossest examples I've experienced is when I visited a "seeker sensitive" church some years ago. The title of the sermon—which still makes me squirm—was, "How to Leverage Your Humility." It was a lesson in how to make best use of humility to get what you want out of life. Jesus, of course, had no place in this sermon. There was no call for us to deny ourselves and take up our crosses and follow Jesus along the *via dolorosa*.

Thy Kingdom Come. In late November of 1932, Dietrich was asked to speak at a women's devotional retreat in Potsdam. Calling it "devotional" risks misleading evangelicals in our day. There was no sentimentality, no private spirituality involved in what he chose to say. His subject was "Thy Kingdom Come! The Prayer of the Church for God's Kingdom on Earth." It is a challenging read but delightful.

Shortly after the conference, Dietrich published an essay based on his lecture. The opening line is: "We are otherworldly or we are secularists, but in either case this means that we no longer believe in God's kingdom" (*DBWE* 12:285). That's an intriguing beginning.

When Jesus prayed with his disciples on the night of his arrest, he described his disciples as "in the world, not of it." Jesus said we are in the world but are "protected" in this world (John 17:11f). For nearly a century now, we have tended to see ourselves "in the world" only in a literal, spatial sense. We're stuck on the planet until being delivered into heaven. And in the meantime, we have formed ourselves into an isolated shelter, priding ourselves on not being like the world. This, of course, is a self-imposed delusion.

Jesus also said very specifically that he has *sent* us into the world (John 17:18). We have a mission here, a God-given purpose, and it is a great deal more than merely preparing us for heaven. When we seek God's protection in this world without accepting our mission to the world, we end up creating spiritual ghettoes for ourselves. We create protective bubbles to protect ourselves from being tainted by the world. However, as every escapist community has found throughout history, we simply bring the world with us into the walled community.

Walk through almost any Christian bookstore; listen to almost any Christian radio station; watch something like the TBN network on television: In all these you'll see the bubble, you'll see Christians busily confirming to one another that they've got the Christian life mastered, but you will rarely hear a mention of the "world" except in a disparaging sense.

Jesus' prayer is different. It doesn't suggest that we are temporarily stuck in this nasty world while we await deliverance but that we are deliberately sent into the world with a mission.

Our desire to be otherworldly, untouched by this real world, leads to mere religion. In a devilish irony, those who try hardest to be other-worldly end up being quite unlike Jesus Christ, whose path led him ever more deeply into the world, not away from it. He was crucified not for leading his followers out of the world but directly into its heart, where the clash was deadly. So the real danger for us is that we might succumb not to "godlessness or cultural Bolshevism at all, but the Christian renunciation of God as the Lord of the Earth" (*DBWE* 12:287).

> Whoever evades the Earth finds not God but only another world, his own better, lovelier, more peaceful world. He finds a world beyond to be sure, but never God's world, which is dawning in this world. Whoever evades Earth in order to find God finds only himself. Whoever evades God in order to find the Earth does not find the Earth as God's Earth. . . (*DBWE* 12:288).

By "earth" Bonhoeffer means all the planet and its inhabitants but especially the world of human society and culture. When we seek some sort of relationship with God which delivers us from the world, we are seeking him where he is not. He has created the earth and blessed the world. In Christ he has planted himself in the same soil of which we ourselves are formed. His cross was driven into the same soil on which we walk every day. What we are called to seek is not God's kingdom outside the world but in the world.[29]

In listening to Bonhoeffer's warning against evading the world, we would do well to notice Paul's word to the Colossians:

> Set your minds on things that are above, not on things that are on earth, for you have died, and your life is hidden with Christ in God. Put to death, therefore, whatever in you is earthly: fornication, impurity, passion, evil desire, and greed (which is idolatry). . . . As God's chosen ones, holy and beloved, clothe yourselves with compassion, kindness, humility, meekness, and patience. Bear

with one another and, if anyone has a complaint against another, forgive each other; just as the Lord has forgiven you, so you also must forgive. Above all, clothe yourselves with love, which binds everything together in perfect harmony.

We are called to have a heavenly mindset, not a mind centered on earthly things. We might think this contradicts Bonhoeffer until we read the rest of what Paul is saying. The heavenly things are compassion, kindness, humility and so on, especially love. The heavenly things, it turns out, are not those things which we have *instead* of the earth. They are the qualities which come from the Spirit of God *to* the earth.

Has not the earth been cursed, according to Genesis 3? Yes, but the curse is not a rejection by God. "Indeed, this is the true curse that is a burden upon the ground of the Earth; not that it yields thistles and thorns. But rather that it hides God's countenance, so that even the deepest furrows in the Earth do not unveil for us the hidden God" (*DBWE* 12:289). It is here, in our own world and in our own context, physical and cultural, that we seek the God who wills to be found. It is here, and here alone, that is our mission field.

What we see, then, in this period of Bonhoeffer's life is that he continues to move toward both the pulpit and toward the lectern. He is seeking a balance of the academic and the pastoral, the theological and the practical. Rather than doing poorly at both, he is already blending the two in very unique ways. As a young man on the way toward a career as a professor, he is shaping his classes in very pastoral ways. As a fellow heading toward a career in the church, he is maintaining the very highest academic standards in his teaching and writing. He is a pastoral professor and an academically astute pastor.

And there is more. We turn next to see that a third dimension is about to be added to his life, that of active resistor against the evils of Hitler and the Nazis.

Endnotes

1. *DBWE* 11:378.
2. *Portrait*, quoting a letter from Dietrich Bonhoeffer to his twin, Sabine, 7 Nov. 1930, 63.

3   Years later he wrote that he had "experienced a year [in America] that has been of the greatest significance for me up to the present day." Letter of 5 Nov 1942, *DBWE* 16: 207.

4   It could have been said at the time that the liberals were engaged with questions only of social justice, while the Fundamentalists lived in a world of merely individual ethics.

5   One of Dietrich's professors at Union, John Baille, later wrote that Bonhoeffer had been "as stout an opponent of liberalism as had ever come my way" (cited in *DB* 158). However, Baille also noted that Bonhoeffer's position differed from liberalism, not by being like the Fundamentalists but by being more Barthian.

6   Oddly enough, the great crisis in America, the crash of the stock market a year before his arrival, seems hardly to have attracted Dietrich's attention. It may be that he was so accustomed to the miserable economic situation in Germany that what he saw in America simply paled in comparison.

7   Initiated and funded primarily by John D. Rockefeller Jr., Riverside's first official service was in October 1930, just two weeks after Bonhoeffer's arrival in New York.

8   "Report on My Year of Study at Union Theological Seminary in New York, 1930/31." *DBWE* 10:315.

9   "After Ten Years," in *DBWE* 8:52.

10 Schlingensiepen learned from Dietrich's youngest sister Susanne that the "view from below" may not have been as new to Dietrich as we might think. Schlingensiepen says, "In their make-believe games, the three youngest were 'always poor people, never kings or counts or fairies.' A special favourite was the 'criminal who is converted' (p. 10).

11 See Bonhoeffer's essay, *Thy Kingdom Come*, in which he writes, "God intends to be Lord on earth and regards all exuberant human zeal on his behalf to be a real disservice" (*DBWE* 12:288).

12 Introduction to *Creation and Fall, DBWE* 3:6.

13 *Creation and Fall, DBWE* 3:50.

14 R. K. McGregor Wright, *No Place for Sovereignty* (InterVarsity Press, 1996). The foreword by Alan Myatt, complains that "war has been declared against any form of Calvinism" (page 7) and commends this book as a good counter attack.

15 R. K. M. Wright, *No Place for Sovereignty* (Westmont, Illinois: InterVarsity Press, 1996), 50.

16 B. F. Skinner, *Beyond Freedom and Dignity* (Cambridge, Massachusetts: Hackett Publishing Company, Inc., 1971).

17 Letter of 22 April 1944: "There are people who change, and many who can hardly change at all. I don't think I have ever changed much, except perhaps at the time of my first impressions abroad, and under the first conscious influence of Papa's personality. It was then that a turning from the phraseological to the real ensued" (*DBWE* 8:358).

18 Francis Schaeffer (1912-1984) was perhaps the most logical, philosophical American apologist, arguing for one of his favorite phrases, "propositional revelation", whereby the attributes of God are revealed as truths or facts that are irrefutable and beyond any doubt, reason or discussion based on the doctrine of Scripture being revealed by God's own Spirit. It is, therefore, doctrine-centered revelations.

19 Yes, I know that non-evangelical readers might well be questioning my claim that evangelicalism has a strong rationalistic strain to it, since much of what evangelicals believe seems utterly irrational to others. Remember, though, that the rational/logical process only moves from presupposition to conclusion. It is the presuppositions which make evangelical thought seem irrational. Many evangelicals work hard to prove their work rational and logical.

20 Clifford Green, in his introduction to *Ethics* (*DBWE* 5:4) notes that, "Here Bonhoeffer interprets the image of God as *imago relationis*, an image of relationship; that is, the image of God is not an attribute possessed by an individual alone, such as reason, but a *particular relationship with others*. A relationship in which a person is free for the other reflects, or images, the freedom of God for humanity in Jesus Christ."

21 C. S. Lewis makes this same point in *Beyond Personality*, usually published as Part Three of *Mere Christianity*. He says people who see us as somehow being absorbed into the divine being misunderstand our communion with God. "They say it is like a drop of water slipping into the sea. But of course that is the end of the drop." Paragraph 3 of chapter two, "The Three-Person God."

22 The new and better translation, of course, is found in *DBWE* 12:299ff, where it is titled merely "Lectures on Christology."

23 The rise of Hitler and his tyranny will be detailed in Chapter Three.

24 Joel Lawrence, *Bonhoeffer: A Guide for the Perplexed* (New York: T & T Clark, 2010), 5.

25 *Teaching a Stone to Talk*, 40.

26 Robert McAfee Brown, *Unexpected News: Reading the Bible with Third World Eyes* (Louisville, Kentucky: Westminster Press, 1984), 15: "There is a primary naïveté that accepts everything in Scripture at face value and digs in its heels when portions of the Bible threaten to be eroded by the acids of modernity." Brown says he works at a critical level but, "After all that critical scrutiny, however, we have returned to the text itself, looking at it with a secondary naïveté, for we still have to ask the pesky question of the text as it stands, 'What does the passage say to us?'" Walter Brueggemann, *Abiding Astonishment*, (Louisville, Kentucky: Westminster John Knox Press, 1991), 41, is even more emphatic: "The mode of objectivity [practiced in critical scholarship] thus embraced is the practice of 'autonomous reason.' . . . The problem with this kind of 'objectivity' and its autonomous reason is that, in the end, 'the autonomy of reason' is linked to 'the autonomy of power.'" Indeed, it is sometimes comical to watch scholars try so hard to make clear that they doubt everything. The ability to dismiss

something is a form of power over the text and, as Brueggemann is suggesting, often leads to a sense of power over all who are more naive and actually believe. Brueggemann returns to this idea in *Interpretation and Obedience*, 28: "We are now in crisis because we are learning that not only are the certitudes we thought 'objectively true' not objective they likely are exercises in control that characteristically tilt toward domination."

27 I never cease to be fascinated by the opening paragraphs of Calvin's great work, *Institutes of the Christian Religion*. We can begin our theological explorations, he says, by examining the human heart. "No one can look upon himself without immediately turning his thoughts to the contemplation of God in whom he 'lives and moves' (Acts 17:28)." Again, ". . . the knowledge of ourselves, not only arouses us to seek God, but also, as it were, leads us by the hand to find him." Yet, he argues, we cannot actually know ourselves without a knowledge of God. "As a consequence, we must infer that man is never sufficiently touched and affected by the awareness of his lowly state until he has compared himself with God's majesty." So he begins his systematic theology with a study of the character of God, if only because "the order of right teaching requires that we discuss the former [God] first, then proceed afterward to treat the latter [humankind]." (Quotations from *Institutes of the Christian Religion*, Vol. XX, Book I [Louisville, Kentucky: Westminster Press, Library of Christian Classics], 35-39.)

28 George Barna, *User Friendly Churches* (Ventura, California: Regal Books, 1997), 107.

29 Whatever else we may say about how radical Bonhoeffer sounds later in his *Letters and Papers*, we cannot pretend that his thoughts in prison were new to him. He did not become more radical than he was in *Thy Kingdom Come*.

CHAPTER THREE

The Rise of Hitler and the Nazis

"Leaders or offices which set themselves up as gods, mock God." [1]

The Great War, now called World War I, had been an extended battle of attrition with neither side willing to admit their forces were locked in a deadly stalemate. The late entrance of the American forces tipped the scales in favor of England and France, but even so it seemed the end was not in sight after four years of bloodshed.

Germany after the War

Germany was the first to blink, suggesting an armistice which was signed on November 11, 1918. Germany, though, never considered itself to have surrendered.[2] Six months later, on June 28, 1919, the Treaty of Versailles was signed, officially ending the war but creating a new level of animosity among the Germans. It was a severely punitive treaty which made German recovery nearly impossible. The French, still stinging from their loss to Germany in the Franco-Prussian War of 1870, demanded Germany pay such huge reparations that Germany's economy, already in shambles, was immediately ruined.[3]

Meanwhile, the tensions and strains of the Great War had turned the political institutions of Germany into shambles. As early as October 1918, efforts were made to create a parliamentary democracy akin to that in England. The Communists, inspired by the 1917 revolutions in Russia, were agitating against democracy, though they lacked the numbers and influence needed to sway Germany toward communism.

Kaiser Wilhelm II abdicated under pressure on November 9, 1918, two days before the armistice. It was not until August 11, 1919, that a new constitution was created and the Weimar Republic established. This was a time of great confusion and mutual antagonism among the German people.

Though a period of relative economic stability was achieved by 1924, it came at the cost of severely increasing the national debt because most of the money stabilizing the economy was in the form of loans from American banks. When the American stock market crashed in 1929, Germany's still-fragile economy was again ruined and its political situation was thrown into worse disarray than ever.[4]

The Appointment of Hitler

There were many in Germany, Adolf Hitler among them, who blamed the Jews for the German capitulation to the enemy at the end of the Great War. This was referred to as the *Dolchstosslegende*, the "stab in the back" legend. Now they added to the charges against the Jews that they had led Germany into economic disaster. While many of Germany's leading citizens and politicians were Jewish, the charge that they were the creators of the problems was completely irrational. Hitler exploited the racial prejudice as a means of gaining power for himself and as his voice grew louder, everything Jewish became targeted for scorn. The Old Testament, for instance, was dismissed as merely Jewish.

One oddity was that Hitler and many of the Nazi leaders embraced an alternative to "Jewish" physics: the World Ice Theory. The idea was that an amateur scientist, Hans Hörbiger, had come up with a better description of the universe than had that Jewish fellow, Albert Einstein. Hörbiger's view was that the planets, stars, and even the moon were solid ice. It may have been a foolish idea but at least it wasn't Jewish, so Hitler planned to make it the official position of the Third Reich.[5]

In such times, of course, there are many people and parties vying for power. Power vacuums always lead to power struggles. The Communists were gaining strength during the twenties and the Nazis began a counter movement. The German president was the popular Paul von Hindenburg, who was 85 when elected to a second term as president in 1932. He was strongly anti-Communist and anti-Nazi but he was also very aged and very weak. He had run only as a way of keeping Hitler from winning the office in the 1932 elections.

The actual leadership of the country was in the hands of the chancellor, a position somewhat like that of prime minister in England. After the economic crash of 1929, Hindenburg appointed a series of chancellors, all of whom failed and resigned. Finally, he could see no choice but to accede to the demands of the brash young Nazi, Adolf Hitler, appointing him chancellor on the afternoon of January 30, 1933. Hindenburg despised Hitler but admitted that at least he was against the Communists and he certainly seemed confident that he could save Germany. No one else had such confidence.

There were some in Germany, the Bonhoeffer family among them, who had already recognized that Germany's hunger for a strong leader made the country ripe for a dictator. And they could see that Hitler was prepared to take full advantage of the situation. From the very first day of his appointment,[6] January 30, 1933, Hitler assumed nearly dictatorial power.[7]

By coincidence, Dietrich Bonhoeffer had prepared a radio message to be delivered on February 1.[8] In that message he tried to warn Germany of the danger of a leader who values power more than justice. Bonhoeffer knew that in hard times people tend to want someone—anyone—to take responsibility for them. He knew that the people were longing, in effect, for a tangible "god" to protect them and he knew that such a man was waiting in the wings. "Leaders or offices," Bonhoeffer said, "which set themselves up as gods mock God. . ." (*DBWE* 12:282).

Unfortunately, he was building carefully toward that warning when he was cut off the air. He had planned too long a message![9] But the gauntlet had been thrown down, and Bonhoeffer's life would never be the same. From that day forward, his whole life was shaped by his opposition to Adolf Hitler.

We might expect that the three German civil institutions with the greatest power to resist and contain Hitler's evil would be the *Reichstag* (parliament), the church, and the university. These in fact proved to be Hitler's easiest and quickest conquests. Note how quickly he gained their submission in a matter of months in 1933.

January 30	Hindenburg appointed Hitler as chancellor.
February 27	The burning of the *Reichstag* building (very possibly on Hitler's order) gave Hitler the excuse to declare martial law, effectively by-passing parliament in future decisions.
March 24	Full dictatorial power granted to Hitler by the puppet parliament.

April 1	The Nazi's call for a one-day boycott of all Jewish businesses.
April 5	"German Christians" demand "synchronization of church and state" (*Gleichschaltung*).
April 7	Parliament, by Hitler's command, issued civil service regulations, including the "Aryan Clause" forbidding Jews from holding civil service positions, presumably, but not clearly, including positions in the churches.
April 25	Hitler appoints a former military chaplain and long-time Nazi—Ludwig Müller—to be his "advisor" on church affairs.
May 10	Largest of several book-burnings to rid Germany of "un-Germanic" influences.
July 20	Hitler and the Catholic church sign a Concordat by which he is bound not to interfere with church matters and the church is not to be critical of state matters.
September 27	The last of the regional synods, all now dominated by the "German Christians," accepts the imposition of Müller as Reich Bishop.

Where were the professors? Many, including some of the leading professors of theology and Bible, quickly spoke out in favor of Hitler as a strong leader and in approval of the nazification of the universities. Among the leading ecclesiastical scholars voicing approval of Hitler's reign were Paul Althaus, prominent in Luther studies; Gerhard Kittel, specialist in Judaic studies; and theologian Emanuel Hirsch.[10]

In 1934, several prominent theologians had responded to the rising Confessing Church and its Barmen Confession by issuing the "Ansbach Memorandum, which reads in part, "The law, 'the unchangeable will of God' . . . obligates us to the natural orders to which we are subject, such as family, people [*volk*], race (that is, blood relationship)" (*DBWE* 6:56).

Hitler had announced years earlier, in *Mein Kampf*, that he was committed to "dealing with" the Jews. It ought to have come as no surprise to the Germans, then, that just a month after Hitler became chancellor, the Nazis called for a one day boycott of Jewish businesses. And, just a month after that, Hitler began his campaign against the Jews by banning them from the civil service. Like all effective tyrants, and more than a few leaders even in the free world, Hitler knew that his leadership would escape serious criticism so long as he kept people's attention on an enemy, real or imagined.

Hitler and the Nazis had an endless capacity for bald-faced lies and most people in Germany and throughout the West placed hope in his vision, minimizing the time when the truth was stretched. British Prime Minister Neville Chamberlain and Pope Pius XI were not the only who trusted Hitler. As late as 1939, in the Gottesburg Declaration, the Nazi-dominated German Christians were claiming,

> National Socialism continues the work of Martin Luther on the ideological and political side, and thus helps, in its religious aspects, the recovery of a true understanding of the Christian faith. . . . The Christian faith is the unbridgeable religious contrast to Judaism.[11]

The deception was still being carried on because, even at that late date, there were many in Germany who believed that if the Nazis said they wanted "a true understanding of the Christian faith," it must be true.

We might want to pause for a moment to remind ourselves how very similar—yet strikingly different—were the stories of Germany and the United States during these years. The economic disaster that hit Germany in 1929 originated in the United States, which was itself thrown into the most serious Depression in its history. The well-intentioned president, Herbert Hoover, was simply not up to the task of rebuilding either the economy or the morale of the people.

In November 1932, Franklin Delano Roosevelt defeated Hoover in the presidential election. He took office on March 4, 1933, and, like Hitler, began working immediately to persuade his people that there was great cause for optimism. "The only thing we have to fear," he proclaimed in his inaugural address, "is fear itself."[12]

Roosevelt did not delay taking the necessary steps for economic reform, beginning with his March 5 bank closures to halt the run on the banks. Observers quickly invented a whole new category for evaluating a presidency: "the first one hundred days." In those hundred days, Roosevelt substantially increased government spending in order to create jobs, issued countless regulations to control the recklessness of the banking and finance industries, and took a host of other measures—many by executive order—to stabilize the economy.

In Germany during that same period, Hitler was raising the broken morale by many of the same measures but also by intimidating and imprisoning any who expressed doubt or criticism. He loudly proclaimed with great, even spectacular fanfare, that he was going to make Germany great again. He increased government spending, creating jobs by building an army. And—as we have seen—he named a "common enemy" to unite the people: the Jews.

The Church and the Jewish Question

In April 1933, in response to the infamous Aryan Clause (banning Jews from civil service), Bonhoeffer wrote an essay entitled "The Church and the Jewish Question." In it he reveals first that he, like nearly all Germans of his day, had such a high regard for the state that the thought of opposing the government was almost impossible to consider. Yet, a contempt of the Jews, always simmering just beneath the surface of German society, was being inflamed by Hitler's rhetoric, actions, and enactments. Bonhoeffer forced himself to envision responsible action against the state if necessary.

Bonhoeffer, like most of his fellow Germans, was steeped in a cultural environment that was emphatic about a citizen's responsibility to the state and, more generally, to authority. They had tried being a democratic republic for awhile at the end of the Great War but the experiment was a complete failure. Hitler seemed the only one who could promise to return Germany, to what seemed to the people, to be the normal state of authority.

In order to consider opposing Hitler and the Nazis, a German citizen needed to reach deeply within his or her own psyche to find a sense of morality that ran deeper than—and counter to—that which had been taught by tradition.

In our own American tradition, we have an interesting example of someone reaching this foundation-deeper-than-tradition in one of our favorite stories, Mark Twain's *Huckleberry Finn*. Huck and a runaway slave named Jim have become friends, though Huck is troubled by his conscience. He knows that a slave is rightfully owned by a master and that therefore he, Huck, should turn Jim in to the authorities. In accordance with all he has been taught by culture and by Christians about right and wrong, he writes a letter in betrayal of his friend. Then he pauses to consider what he is doing. As he says later:

> I took it up, and held it in my hand. I was atrembling, because I'd got to decide, forever, betwixt two things, and I knowed it. I studied a minute, sort of holding my breath, and then says to myself: "All right, then, I'll go to hell' and tore it up.[13]

Morality, Huck is learning, is about something deeper than the rules we've been taught and grown accustomed to. It is one of the tasks of the church--isn't it?--to help Christ's followers to discern this "something deeper." Instead, we are very busily engaged in trying to imitate our culture so that people won't have to change to feel happy in our midst. When do we call them to become counter-cultural, to become like Christ? When do we call them to reject all racism, all anti-Semitism, all hatred of anyone different?

Is Huck Finn not your favorite guide to morality? Then perhaps we can attend for a moment to one of the shapers of the modern evangelical movement, C. S. Lewis. In *Mere Christianity*, one of the most popular books as evangelicalism was being formed in the 1950s and 60s, Lewis speaks of our deepest moral instincts, such as love of family, and argues that there is a moral law which stands outside us and guides our decisions about how we are to evaluate our deepest moral instincts. "There is none of our impulses which the moral law may not sometimes tell us to suppress, and none which it may not sometimes tell us to encourage."[14] What is right in one situation, in other words, may not be right in another.

Stating the matter in an even more challenging way, Lewis writes:

> Strictly speaking, there are no such things as good and bad impulses. Think once again of a piano. It has not got two kinds of notes on it, the "right" notes and the "wrong" ones. Every single note is right at one time and wrong at another. The Moral Law is not any one instinct or any set of instincts: it is something which makes a kind of tune (the tune we call goodness or right conduct) by directing the instincts.[15]

Back now to Bonhoeffer's essay on the "Jewish question."[16] He was forced to speak in strong terms, though today we might think them not strong enough. He said the church must resist state domination, first by questioning the legitimacy of state actions which violate its God-given limits and second by serving the victims of illegitimate state action. He clearly has the Jews in mind and is therefore making a startling call on the church to take care of the Jews. And then he wrote, "The third possibility is not just to bind up the wounds of the victims beneath the wheel but to seize the wheel itself" (*DBWE* 12:365). We use "seize" here in the now less common sense of causing the parts to become stuck or bound. He is saying we are to act to stop the state from harming its own people. Little could he have guessed that such words would someday lead him to participation in a conspiracy to assassinate the head of state.

Many evangelicals, stuck in the paralysis that followed the infamous Scopes' trial and the failure of Prohibition, are very leery of those who work for "social justice." Glenn Beck, opening an interview with Eric Metaxas, said, "The Left likes to take Dietrich Bonhoeffer and say that he is, um, a social justice guy. [Eric's] book says, No, not so much."[17] One wonders how one can "seize the wheel" without being engaged in working for social justice. There are some evangelicals who seem to confuse social justice for social*ism*, but if we are not acting toward the issues of social justice (the poor, the helpless, the disenfranchised, the neglected) how can one "bind up the wounds?"

The Bethel Confession and the Confessing Church

By the end of the summer of 1933, Hitler had emasculated the parliament, the universities, and the churches.[18] There were no institutions left to limit his dictatorial and brutal ways. Those which we might expect to have been Hitler's greatest opponents were his earliest and easiest conquests.

Bonhoeffer was one of the most active voices in calling on the church to resist the tyranny but there were many others. He and Herman Sasse, another of the younger theologians beginning to work against the nazification of the church, were asked by Pastor Martin Niemöller and others to draft a statement affirming the freedom of the church from state domination. The fundamental issue was defined by Bonhoeffer in a letter to his grandmother Julie, written in August as work was proceeding on a new confession of faith. He wrote, "The issue is really Germanism or Christianity, and the sooner the conflict comes out in the open, the better" (*DBWE* 12:159). He already could see that the enemy of the church was Germany's love of itself.[19]

The initial draft of the "Bethel Confession" (so named because that's where Bonhoeffer and others created that first draft) had been bold and clear in calling the state (i.e., Hitler) to justice. The final draft, however, was badly diluted by compromises demanded by the more timid members of the Confessing Church. They feared angering Hitler and could not conceive of the church calling the state to justice. Such a bold idea seemed to violate Luther's teaching about the separation of church and state. Thus, the Bethel Confession was to have no effect even on those Christians who disliked Hitler. Bonhoeffer himself chose not to sign the weakened statement.

One of the key concerns motivating a new confession was Hitler's insistence that Jewish Christians be excluded not only from civil service but also from church leadership.[20] Though Bonhoeffer was deeply opposed to the antisemitism that was so thoroughly ingrained in many German minds, he and most of the others felt constrained to address the matter in a limited way, at least in the beginning. The issue they dealt with was the duty of the church, under the Lordship of Christ, to resist domination by the state, especially when it is led by a *Führer* who is himself competing with Christ for lordship over the people.

It seems in hindsight that even the most astute among them were still so very devoted to the Germanic *Volk*, the Germanic heritage, and so provincial, that they wanted to be careful to stay within the accepted boundaries of their accustomed sphere of authority. A common interpretation of Luther's doctrine of Two Kingdoms, whatever he had meant to suggest, had become deeply ingrained in the German mind as an idea that church and state were entirely separate realms, with neither having jurisdiction over the other.

Complicating matters, of course, was the fact that anti-Semitism had long been part of the dark underside of Germany. "It was usually in the name of Luther that the voice of the Church in Germany was almost totally silent on the Jewish question."[21]

This put the church in a very weak position when Hitler rejected the idea of separation of church and state. The church, he insisted, was completely like all other institutions under the sovereignty of the state. He began immediately to dominate the church. The church continued trying to honor the arrangement by speaking in opposition only in the rarest of circumstances. This had the effect of granting Hitler permission to destroy the church. We will see later, when we examine the conspiracy that cost the lives of Bonhoeffer and many others, that the desire to sustain traditional Germanic values was a serious hindrance to the work of the conspirators.

Loyalty and obedience were intrinsic values in the hearts of the Germans. The paradigm shift they needed was far greater than most Westerners can imagine.

One of the obvious lessons to be learned from this is that if injustice is to be recognized and resisted, it will be by those who have been practicing justice all along. Being at best tolerant of anti-Semitism for so very long made it nearly impossible for most Germans to recognize and resist the evil extremes of Hitler's thinking. This was as true of the Christians as of any other Germans. Sadly, it has also been true of a great many other peoples for the past two thousand years.

Years later, Eberhard Bethge, in reflecting on the early experiences of the Confessing Church, said, "We were resisting by way of confession, but we were not confessing by way of resistance."[22] It is not for us who stand at a safe distance to throw a stone or even a pebble at the Confessing Christians. We can only observe with Bethge that the movement from confession to action proved too difficult for all but a handful of the people.

They wanted peace and recognized that Hitler was the enemy of peace. Bonhoeffer, though unheeded, tried to teach them how to work toward real peace. In a sermon delivered at an ecumenical conference on the island of Fanø, Denmark, in the summer of 1934, Bonhoeffer challenged the participants with these strong words:

> How does peace come about? Through a system of political treaties? Through the investment of international capital in different countries? Through the big banks, through money? Or through universal peaceful rearmament in order to guarantee peace? Through none of these, for the single reason that in all of them peace is confused with safety. There is no way to peace along the way of safety. For *peace must be dared*. It is the great venture. It can never be made safe. Peace is the opposite of security. To demand guarantees is to mistrust, and this mistrust in

turn brings forth war (*DBWE* 13:308f; emphasis added).

Try as they might, the pastors of the Confessing and ecumenical churches could find no way to limit the abuses of Hitler without risking his retaliation. One does not defang an adder without irritating the adder.

Many in the Confessing Church reasoned that the task of the church was to preach the Gospel, not reform the political powers. Bethge notes that:

> Hitler never forbade the preaching of that kind of Gospel. He never dared to—why should he? It didn't matter to him whether that was proclaimed or not. Forgiveness of sins was preached in such a way that the whole thing petered out into nothingness. The word about God's justice over against man was not taken in its very literal sense, and thus the original words lost their power to upset people, or may I put it very crudely, the continual preaching of individualistic salvation became a robbery in our country.[23]

A Pastoral Call

Deeply discouraged by his inability to motivate the church leaders, Bonhoeffer accepted a pastorate in London in the fall of 1933.[24] He stayed engaged in ecumenical matters and remained in touch with friends and family in Germany, but for the most part he was simply in retreat. In a letter to Barth, Bonhoeffer shows that he was experiencing something of an identity crisis. Explaining the move to England, he wrote:

> I no longer felt inwardly equal to the questions and demands that I was facing. I felt that, in some way I don't understand, I found myself in radical opposition to all my friends; I was becoming increasingly isolated with my views of the matter, even though I was and remain personally close to these people. . . . [T]here seemed no particular reason why my own view in these matters should be any better, any more right, than the views of many really good and able pastors whom I sincerely respect (*DBWE* 13:23).

Who am I, he seemed to be asking, that I should think my understanding is greater than that of other sincere, respected individuals? This seems to be his first period of serious self-doubt. The second would come years later when he briefly escaped to America in 1939 before deciding he must suffer with others in Germany if he were to have the right to work with them in rebuilding the church after the war.

From London he remained in active communication with the resisting pastors, returning to Germany every six to eight weeks. He was one of the initial supporters of the May 1934 Barmen Declaration, a second and more successful attempt to establish the doctrinal foundations of a church free from state domination. It had been written primarily by Karl Barth who, though Swiss, had been a professor in Germany. Bonhoeffer agreed with the need for such a declaration, even though not completely satisfied with the final outcome.

The Barmen Declaration of 1934

This document was the foundation of the Confessing Church. It was that which the pastors *confessed* together and which therefore united them. The declaration spoke strongly against the subordination of the church to the state, insisting that the church answers to no one but the Lord himself. With Karl Barth as its primary author, the declaration had to be approved by the larger Confessing Church before becoming a definitive statement of the church's confession. In the process of gaining that approval, a number of modifications were made by various Lutheran theologians and leaders. Many of the changes had to do with strengthening the declaration's reflection of the very ideas it was designed to resist, especially in the area of the two-state theology of Luther. After just a year as chancellor, Hitler had already frightened so many people in Germany that even a statement of resistance, many thought, had to be carefully worded so as not to offend Hitler.

As a result of those changes and of his own failure in the original document to address Nazi antisemitism, the issue of the Jews in Germany, even Barth was disappointed in the weakness of the declaration. Nonetheless, the Barmen Declaration was the best the Confessing Church could agree on at the time. It did have its desired effect of giving to the new church a strong though not broad foundation.

Though increasingly aware that Hitler had to be resisted, Bonhoeffer continued giving his primary attention to the church, especially now the Confessing Church. He had already declared the Nazi-dominated German Church to be not a church at all.[25] He had been quite bold in his opposition to Hitler and in calling upon his fellow Christians to resist the tyranny that was beginning to grip the nation.

In 1935, at the age of only 29, he returned from England at the request of the Confessing Church to establish and direct a new seminary, one of five authorized by the Confessing Church through its Dahlem Synod. Unlike our American educational system, in Germany future pastors first received their theological education at a university and then attended a seminary only for about a year of practical training in the rubrics of their chosen profession. The Confessing Church recognized the need for a better theological seminary training that reflected those commitments which distinguished them from the dominant German Christians.

Contemporizing New Testament Texts

Returning to Germany to begin work with the seminary, Bonhoeffer took the time to deliver a major address to a Confessing Church conference in August. He chose to explore a problem which remains unsolved to our day: How do we preach and teach the Bible in a way that is true to Scripture, cognizant of biblical scholarship, and relevant to the hearers? American evangelicals in the last half-century have devoted a great deal of attention and experimentation on the third of those factors but, I believe, have been negligent of the first two.

Bonhoeffer's lecture, entitled "Contemporizing New Testament Texts" in *DBWE* 14:413 (earlier called "Interpreting New Testament Texts" in English translations), seems to me to be somewhat labored, as if he were thinking the matter through even while talking. This is characteristic of his other writings in the early 30s, such as his essay on "The Church and the Jewish Question" in 1933. We can easily forgive him and even thank him for working so hard to develop a mature theology at such a young age and under such difficult circumstances.

We can also respect him because, however much he may wander in search of the right way to articulate his insights, he does show very clearly that he is firmly grasping his central points. In this case, though he jumps from one metaphor to another, his primary ideas do come through forcefully.

The first and central idea is that, in the necessary attempt to help people make a connection between Scripture and our present day, it is essential that we know what sort of connection is needed. The temptation is always for us to "update" the Bible, to put it into contemporary terms and to choose those parts that suit us. We do the same in our church life, of course, always trying to be relevant. This is unavoidable and not in itself a problem.

In my own life, one of the first steps toward faith was when I was reading the Gospels and realized that this Jesus of two thousand years ago would have been a wonderful man to know. I was convinced that Jesus, were he still alive, would see into my heart and help me to know myself. Only after some months did I understand that the claim of the New Testament was just that: Jesus is alive and present for us.

There is a grave danger, however, of distorting the Gospel merely to suit modern tastes. Henri Nouwen observes that the desire to be relevant, popular, and powerful "are not vocations but temptations."[26]

The first and central emphasis in Bonhoeffer's lecture is emphatic and very challenging to modern evangelical churches. We must beware of the dangers of trying too hard to make the Bible seem "contemporary."

Eugene Peterson, perhaps today's wisest counselor of pastors, warns of letting the role of Christian leaders be defined for us by the culture around us:

> All [culture] asks is that I accept its definition of my work as an encourager of the culture's good will, as the priest who will sprinkle holy water on the culture's good intentions. . . . But if I, even for a moment, accept my culture's definition of me, I am rendered harmless. I can denounce evil and stupidity all I wish and will be tolerated in my denunciations as a court jester is tolerated.[27]

In fact, says Bonhoeffer, we are challenged to do something quite the opposite of trying to fit into whatever slot the culture makes for us.

> The question of contemporizing the New Testament message is basically capable of a dual exposition. Either one understands it to mean that the biblical message must justify itself to the present . . . or that the present must justify itself to the biblical message. . . (*DBWE* 14:415).

What Bonhoeffer had in mind, of course, was the accommodation of Bible and Church to the Nazi domination of German culture. Crosses and swastikas were intermingled in church sanctuaries across the land. Sometimes the swastika was even imprinted on the cross. When preaching or speaking about Jesus, it was an Aryan Jesus, certainly not a Jewish Jesus. And the Old Testament, regarded as Jewish, was dismissed entirely. There was no way in which the German Christians were heeding Bonhoeffer's charge that we are to learn to read Scripture not just *for* ourselves but *against* ourselves (*DBWE* 11:377f). Later, in writing *Life Together*, he will say that "We expose ourselves to the particular sentence and word [of Scripture] until we personally are affected by it" (*DBWE* 5:87). Or, to add a bit of salt to that bland translation, we are to address ourselves to the Bible until it addresses us; we examine it until we realize that, in the light of Scripture, we are the ones being examined.

Millions of dollars each month are being spent by advertisers in America who want very much to convince us that we are entitled to be self-centered. Such a mindset even affects the way we read the Bible, wanting more than anything else to "get something out of it." What Bonhoeffer advocates—and what we evangelicals need to emphasize—is that the greater priority is for God, by way of the Bible and the Spirit of Christ speaking through the Bible, to be getting something out of us: change. We are to be ever changing toward being a more biblical people, a more Christlike people.

The Church completely abandons the prophetic dimension of its call when its first priority is to conform to society. That's a real danger in today's evangelical churches.

For Bonhoeffer the tendency toward accommodation has roots in the Enlightenment, where the devotion to Reason (they always seemed to capitalize it back then) ended up making each thoughtful individual feel as if he or she were the final arbiter of all truth. The irony is that, while the Enlightenment rationalists thought they were thus improving our search for truth, the actual result was quite the opposite. Because one rational mind may reach different conclusions than another, suddenly "truth" becomes relative. Everything depends on what one believes and no one has an ultimate claim to know the truth.[28]

Bonhoeffer saw this elevation of human autonomy as a form of idolatry, the supplanting of God by the individual, who became the Lord of his or her own life. Isn't that what is portrayed for us in the story of Adam and Eve?

The attempt to contemporize the Bible, to adapt and adjust it so that it is easily seen as relevant, too easily becomes a matter of the biblical message being passed "through the sieve of one's own knowledge," (*DBWE* 14:414) with a concomitant disdain for whatever does not match current knowledge or suit present tastes. Thus, to follow Bonhoeffer in a quick switch of metaphors, the eagle with clipped wings can no longer fly. Christianity, thus tamed, is no Christianity at all.

Bonhoeffer says we are not to be overly worried about protecting the Bible from sounding obsolete. We do not need (again switching metaphors) a perfect drinking glass to enjoy the water. He assures us that "those who are thirsty will drink water from whatever vessel is available, be it ever so difficult (*DBWE* 14:416).

It is the task of the preacher not to make the Bible simple but to speak it clearly, trusting the Holy Spirit to convey the message to the heart of the listener. Henri Nouwen pursues much the same line when thinking not just about the Bible but about the preacher or other leader. He writes that ". . . the Christian leader of the future is called to be completely irrelevant and to stand in this world with nothing to offer but his or her own vulnerable self." After all, Nouwen reminds us, "Jesus' first temptation was to be relevant: to turn stones into bread."[29]

Most preachers, I think, are keenly aware of and encouraged by the story of Balaam's ass in Numbers 22. When Balaam was blind to the angel sent by God to stop him from a foolish mission, his donkey spoke to warn him. Preachers, especially just before the sermon, comfort themselves with the thought that, if God could speak through a jackass in those days, he can do it again this very morning. The task is not to strive for success or popularity but simply for a faithful speaking of God's Word.

Three Personal Letters

Bonhoeffer was marked by a stereotypical Prussian reserve about him, a reluctance to reveal himself even to long standing friends, except for Eberhard Bethge. We find three unusually personal letters to be especially valuable as we seek to know Bonhoeffer. They were written in 1935 and 1936, the first shortly before and the second two during his leadership of the Confessing Church seminary, which had come to be known simply as Finkenwalde.

The first letter, dated 14 January 1935, was written from London to his eldest brother, already a well-established professor of chemistry at the University of Leipzig.[30] I must resist the temptation to print the whole letter here, fascinating though it is. Here is the part in which Bonhoeffer reflects on his faith:

> Perhaps I seem to you rather fanatical and mad about a number of things. I myself am sometimes afraid of that. But I know that the day I become more 'reasonable,' to be honest, I should have to chuck my entire theology. When I first started in theology, my idea of it was quite different—rather more academic, probably. Now it has turned into something else altogether. But I do believe that at last I am on the right track, for the first time in my life. I often feel quite happy about it. I only worry about being so afraid of what other people will think as to get bogged down instead of going forward. I think I am right in saying that I would only achieve true inner clarity and honesty by really starting to take the Sermon on the Mount seriously. Here alone lies the force that can blow all this hocus-pocus sky-high—like fireworks, leaving only a few burnt-out shells behind (*DBWE* 13:284).

Bonhoeffer speaks of a change in his theological work. Begun as primarily academic, it has become something much more personal to him. He can no longer study theology "objectively" or academically because he now sees the matter from the inside out, more as a believer than as a mere observer.

The letter also gives us a clue as to when the personal transition took place: it was in discovering the Sermon on the Mount. This came primarily through his friendship with Jean Laserre while at Union Seminary during the 1930-1931 school year. By this time, if not earlier, he had begun the habit of reading the daily selection from a devotion booklet published by the Moravian Brethren.[31]

What he says about the Sermon on the Mount is remarkable. "Here alone lies the force that can blow all this hocus-pocus sky high, like fireworks, leaving only a few burnt-out shells behind." The hocus-pocus is Hitler and the Nazi takeover of the government. The weapon to destroy it, he believes, is simply the Sermon on the Mount. There is a power which is greater even than Hitler's.

I must admit that in my decades as a follower of Jesus Christ, I've never heard anyone ascribe such power to those few chapters of Matthew's Gospel. We've domesticated the Bible to such a degree that it is harmless, merely offering a few tidbits which happen to please us. A power greater than Hitler's? Only if we take the Sermon seriously.

The second letter which tells us something personal about Bonhoeffer was written January 27, 1936, from Finkenwalde to a young woman with whom he had been quite close a bit earlier, Elizabeth Zinn (later the wife of theologian Günther Bornkamm).

> I threw myself into my work in an extremely very un-Christian and not at all humble fashion. A rather crazy element of ambition, which some people noticed in me, made my life difficult. . . . But then something different came, something that has changed and transformed my life to this very day. For the first time I came to the Bible. . . . I had often preached, I had seen a great deal of the church, spoken and preached about it—and yet I was not yet a Christian. . . .
>
> I do know that at that time I turned the cause of Jesus Christ into an advantage for myself, for my crazy vanity. I pray to God that will never happen again. Nor had I ever prayed, or had done so only very rarely. Despite this isolation, I was quite happy with myself. The Bible, especially the Sermon on the Mount, freed me from this. Since then everything has changed. I have felt this plainly and so have other people around me. That was a great liberation. It became clear to me that the life of a servant of Jesus Christ must belong to the church, and step-by-step it became clearer to me how far it must go. Then came the crisis of 1933. This strengthened me in it.
>
> I also met others who shared the same goal. For me everything now depended on a renewal of the church and of the pastoral station. . . (*DBWE* 14:134f).

This sounds to evangelicals like what we would call a conversion experience, though Bonhoeffer himself did not use such language and probably would not have thought of the transformation in quite that way. Again, it was the Bible, and particularly the Sermon on the Mount, that was at the center of Bonhoeffer's change. The fruit of the experience was that he was in a new and apparently more personal sense "a servant of Jesus Christ." Rather than merely rejoicing in the pleasure of the transformation, however, his mind goes immediately to his sense of call from Jesus: he is called to "belong to the church."

The third letter, dated April 8, 1936, in which Bonhoeffer speaks rather personally of himself is written to his brother-in-law, Rüdiger Schleicher. It is a long and captivating letter from which I'll quote just a few lines.

> Let me first admit quite simply: I believe that the Bible alone is the answer to all our questions, and that we merely need ask perpetually and with a bit of humility in order to get the answer from it. One cannot simply read the Bible like other books. One must be prepared genuinely to query it. Only thus does it reveal itself (*DBWE* 14:167).

I cannot begin to tell you the number of times in small group inductive Bible studies I've heard people say something like, "This is a great way to study. In my church we weren't allowed to ask questions." Churches that are centered on answers tend not to value questions, but Bonhoeffer knows that to see and hear the truth in Scripture we must be asking questions—sincere, hard, challenging questions.

Some may worry that, since the Bible is so often criticized, it may not stand up to rigorous questioning. D. L. Moody once said: "Defend the Bible? I'd sooner defend a lion." Deep answers do not come from shallow inquiries. Bonhoeffer again:

> The reason is that God is speaking to us in the Bible. And one cannot simply reflect on God on one's own; one must ask God. Only if we seek God will God answer. Of course, one can also read the Bible just as one does any other book, for example, from the perspective of textual criticism, etc. There can be no objections to such reading. It merely is not the use that genuinely discloses the essence of the Bible; it discloses merely its surface (*DBWE* 14:167).

To miss the heart of God is to miss the heart of Scripture as well. And to miss the heart of Scripture is to be deaf to the Word God is speaking to us through the Bible. Just as a theologian must be a believer to properly understand, so must a student of Scripture be listening for the voice of the Spirit in Bible study. To objectify God or Scripture is to make oneself superior to them, the judge of what is right and wrong with each. Bonhoeffer is deeply convinced that such superiority is a serious flaw.

> Only if we finally dare to come to the Bible assuming that the one speaking to us here really is the God who loves us and has no intention of abandoning us with our questions will we come to rejoice in the Bible (*DBWE* 14:167).

Our security lies not in the Bible itself but in the Lord who stands behind the Bible and is heard through the Bible. The Lord loves us and will not abandon us, no matter how many questions we ask or how many doubts we express. The test of our faith is not whether we do or do not have doubts and unanswered questions. Rather, faith is shown by what we do with our doubts and queries: Do we take them to the Lord or not? Again, Bonhoeffer:

> Either I determine the place where I want to find God, or I let him determine the place where he wants to be found. If it is I who says where God is to be found, then I will always find a God there who in some manner corresponds to me, is pleasing to me, who is commensurate with my own nature. But if it is God who says where he is to be found, then it will probably be a place that is not at a commensurate with my own nature and that does not please me at all. This place, however, is the cross of Jesus. And those who want to find God there must live beneath that cross just as the Sermon on the Mount demands. Doing so, however, is wholly incommensurate with our nature, indeed, is wholly contrary to it. Precisely this, however, is the message of the Bible, not only in the New but also in the Old Testament (Isa. 53!) (*DBWE* 14:168).

It is a consistent theme with Bonhoeffer that the initiative is always the Lord's. We are the responders, not the initiators in our relationship with God. If we seek to reverse the roles, we end up trying to shape the relationship to our own liking. As Bonhoeffer puts it a bit later in the letter, "Every other place outside the Bible has become too uncertain for me. There I am always afraid of encountering merely my own divine *Doppelgänger*" (*DBWE* 14:169).[32] We often criticize the Greeks for having a thoroughly anthropomorphic view of the gods, yet we ourselves are also inclined to describe the Creator of the Universe as if he were just like us, only bigger. The biblical message is quite different: God has created us in his image but, having in some sense skewed the *imago dei* within us, we ought not merely extrapolate from the human heart a picture of the heart of God. Instead, we are to so open ourselves to the work of the Spirit of Jesus Christ that we are "being renewed in knowledge according to the image of [our] creator" (Colossians 3:10).

> And now I really would also like to say to you personally, that since having learned to read the Bible in this way—and it has not been at all that long—it becomes more miraculous to me each day. I read it each morning and evening, often during the day as well, and every day I focus on a text I have chosen for the entire week, trying to immerse myself in it entirely that I may truly hear it. Now know that I could no longer really live properly without this. And I certainly could not believe properly. And increasingly more riddles are becoming clear to me each day; we still seem to cling wholly to the surface of things (*DBWE* 14:169).

Bonhoeffer's love of Scripture clearly shines through here. Later, from prison he would write almost with surprise that his appetite for the Bible would wax and wane, as happens to all of us even without the stress of imprisonment.[33] Yet never did Bonhoeffer waver in his desire to be biblical in his thinking, his desire to think God's thoughts after him.

Endnotes

1 *DBWE* 12:282.

2 See the final chapter for observations on the Germans' attitudes at the conclusion of the Second World War.

3 Amazingly, Germany continued paying these reparations (except during the Hitler era) until October 2010, the twentieth anniversary of the reunification of Germany.

4 The causes of World War II, of course, are quite complex. Following John Maynard Keynes' interpretation, a primary factor is usually considered to be the harsh demands of the Versailles Treaty. Just as important, I believe, is the crash of the stock market, which was even more devastating to Germany than to the US. Roger Kimball, editor of "The New Criterion," believes there was a deeper, underlying problem: Western culture as a whole was in a phase of decomposition that began before World War I. Our understanding of what it means to be human was becoming shattered. Picasso's "Les Demoiselles d'Avignon" in 1907 and Duchamp's

"Nude Descending a Staircase" in 1912 were already showing us that we were in some ugly way distorting, even mechanizing, human nature. Virginia Woolf, says Kimball, saw a 1910 showing of works by post-Impressionist painter Roger Fry and remarked, "On or about December 10, 1910, human character changed." Kimball's idea adds an insightful dimension to our understanding of the complex situation in Germany as the decade of the 1930s began. Cultural change, of course, may set the stage for violence but does not make it inevitable.

5   I confess to not finding the theory worth any research, so I'll just refer the reader to the Wikipedia article called *Welteislehre*.

6   The position of chancellor was filled not by popular election but by presidential appointment by Hindenburg. When Hindenburg died on August 2, 1934, Hitler declared himself president as well as chancellor. He then held an election for himself and won by popular vote on August 19, 1934.

7   A simple but very good exposition of the contemporary context for Bonhoeffer's work in the 1930s is woven throughout *Bonhoeffer for Armchair Theologians*, Stephen R. Haynes and Lori Brandt Hale (Louisville, Kentucky: Westminster John Knox Press, 2009). Also helpful in this regard is the biography by Ferdinand Schlingensiepen, *Dietrich Bonhoeffer, 1906-1945: Martyr, Thinker, Man of Resistance*, English edition (New York: T & T Clark, 2010).

8   "The Führer and the Individual in the Younger Generation," (*DBWE* 12:268). a brief essay summarizing the talk was given to the radio station. It was entitled "The Younger Generation's Altered View of the Concept of Führer," (*DBWE* 12:266).

9   Bethge remained suspicious to the end that the Gestapo had simply cut the broadcast short when they realized where the message was headed (*DB* 260). Bonhoeffer himself, so far as we know, made no such claim. He did write the next day that the message "had gone slightly over time" (*DBWE* 12:91).

10 Robert P. Ericksen, *Theologians under Hitler* (New Haven, Connecticut: Yale University Press, 1985).

11 Cited in Francis I. Andersen, "Dietrich Bonhoeffer and the Old Testament," *Reformed Theological Review*, May-August, 1975, p. 38.

12 This was actually a paraphrase of a line from Francis Bacon, who said, "Nothing is to be feared except fear itself." Cited in Catherine Drinker Bowen, *Francis Bacon: The Temper of a Man* (New York: Fordham University Press, 1993), 221.

13 There are many editions of *Huck Finn*. This quotation is from the section entitled "Ominous Plans."

14 *Mere Christianity*, 22.

15 *Mere Christianity*, 22.

16 I confess to being amazed at how easily the Nazis turned the fact of Germany's Jews into a question, *Judenfrage*. While there had been tensions between the Jews and other Germans, there were a great many Jews among the leading Germans of the day. It was Hitler who created the illusion that the Jews constituted

a serious question which Germany needed to answer. He learned from the serpent: "Did God say you are not to eat of any tree?"

17 YouTube video "Glenn Beck - Eric Metaxas on Bonhoeffer - Pt 1, " https://www.youtube.com/watch?v=-kK1ZK9u7xw

18 Like Barth at the beginning of World War I, Bonhoeffer was deeply offended that some of his own professors quickly showed support for Hitler as being Germany's only hope. Both Barth and Bonhoeffer were convinced that the theology they had been taught was clearly inadequate if it allowed the professors to be so provincial, so narrowly Germanic, that they not only valued Germany over all the rest of the world but even over common morality itself. I remember seeing bumper stickers during the Viet Nam war: "My country, right or wrong." That is a statement of inexcusable spiritual and moral blindness. Bonhoeffer would never accept the idea that we can evade personal responsibility by saying it is the state which is responsible.

19 Karl Barth reflected back on this period in German history and said that "beside the Holy Scriptures as the unique source of revelation, the German-Christians affirm the German nationhood, its history and its contemporary political situation as a second source of revelation, and thereby betray themselves to believers in 'another god.'" Essay: "The Church's Oppositon, 1933" in *The German Church Conflict* (Philadelphia: John Knox Press, 1956) (ET 1965). In the Introduction to *Exile in the Fatherland: Martin Niemöller's Letters from Moabit Prison*, Editor Hubert Locke notes two examples of this Germany-centered thinking. First, he quotes Pastor Joachim Hossenfelder, who said the German Christians were "the S.A. [that is, the brownshirts] of Jesus Christ. . . . We regard as holy these laws of God's creation: marriage, family, race, people, state, and authority." Second, he quotes from a resolution passed by the German Christians in April 1933, which said in part: "God has created me a German. Germanism is a gift of God; God desires that I battle for my Germanism. . . . The church is, for a German, a communion of believers that is duty bound to fight for a Christian Germany. The goal of the German Christian Faith Movement is one evangelical German church. The state of Adolf Hitler calls for such a church; the church must hear that call." (Both quotations are on page 18.)

20 Because pastors were paid by the government, their position was considered a form of civil service.

21 Andersen, Francis I., "Dietrich Bonhoeffer and the Old Testament," *Reformed Theological Review*, May-August 1975: 38. Andersen adds: "It is to Bonhoeffer's everlasting credit that he saw where all this was going quite clearly from the first, and never wavered in his opposition to every non-Aryan move made by the Reich."

22 Bethge, Eberhard, *Friendship and Resistance: Essays on Dietrich Bonhoeffer* (Geneva: WCC Publications and Grand Rapids: Wm. B. Eerdmans Publishing Co., 1995), 24.

23 Eberhard Bethge, *Prayer and Righteous Action*, Christian Journals, Ltd, 1979, 16f. Perhaps Bethge is suggesting that the focus on individual salvation robs the

church of its rightful role in standing for justice. To glance at the prophets, especially Amos, is to see that social justice is of fundamental concern to God.

24 Because so much attention has been devoted to Bonhoeffer in the last half-century, we easily forget that he actually had little influence in Germany, even in the Confessing Church, in his own day. As Victoria Barnett observes, "Although he was enormously loved and respected by his students, the rest of the church disregarded him. Many Confessing Christians never heard of Bonhoeffer until after 1945." "Dietrich Bonhoeffer's Ecumenical Vision," *Christian Century*, April 26, 1995: 454.

25 *DBWE* 14:675f. He writes, "Whoever knowingly separates himself from the Confessing Church in Germany separates himself from salvation."

26 Henri Nouwen, *In the Name of Jesus* (New York: Crossroads Publishing Co., 1993), 71.

27 Eugene Peterson, *The Contemplative Pastor* (Grand Rapids: Wm. B. Eerdmans Publishing Co., 1993), 24.

28 The first chapter of Ericksen's *Theologians under Hitler* is a good exposition of the twentieth century's despair of finding intellectual truth.

29 Henri Nouwen, *In the Name of Jesus* (New York: Crossroads Publishing Co., 1993).

30 He later became director of the Kaiser Wilhelm Institute and then the Max Planck Institute for Physical Chemistry, now called the Karl Friedrich Bonhoeffer Institute.

31 *The Daily Watchword* (*Losungen* in German) has been published annually since 1731. It is still in use by more than 1.5 million people around the globe and can be found online at www.moravian.org. It is most likely, of course, that Bonhoeffer learned of this through his mother. In this, as in so many ways, Bonhoeffer is like the Pietists, though he did not like what he saw of the Pietists in Germany. They were too individualistic in their faith and yet too public in sharing that faith.

32 A look-alike or double of oneself.

33 Letter to Bethge, 25 June 1942: "I am amazed that I am living, and can live, for days without the Bible. When I then open my Bible again, it is new and delightful to me as never before, and I only wish I could preach again" (*DBWE* 16:329).

CHAPTER FOUR

The Seminary at Finkenwalde

Never speak about another person in that person's absence or else tell that person about it immediately afterward.[1]

It was clear that the Confessing Church, which had evolved into what we might call a separate denomination in opposition to the German Christians, needed to provide pastoral training if its congregations were to have leadership in their new direction. To do this they sought to establish five seminaries, with Bonhoeffer invited to lead one of them.

The Seminary

Classes for Bonhoeffer's students began in late April 1935. In a certain sad irony, this was the same year that Hitler's devious ways began to have a suppressing effect on the Confessing Church. With the July establishiment of the Ministry of Church Affairs, the year 1935 was both the best time for the Confessing Church and simultaneously the year in which it began to unravel. The students who were sent or drawn to the new seminary knew that at the very least they were risking the disapproval of the Nazis, yet they must have been shocked to find their new leader even more radical than they. Their young teacher stood in marked opposition to the German state church—which took the name "German Christians"—and even stronger contrast to the government officials who were trying to bring the church entirely under state control. The Nazis called their intended domination of the church "coordination" (*Gleichshaltung*).

Bonhoeffer threw himself into the task with great joy, having the sense that at last he had found the perfect balance between a life of scholarship and pastoral ministry. What he created was a seminary with very high academic standards but with the Bible itself at the core of the curriculum. The Bible was the source of the content of the school, not merely a part of a curriculum of the history of the church.

The school was more than an academy: it was a community almost monastic in its disciplines.² In fact, Bonhoeffer borrowed a great deal from the experiences of Protestant monasteries he had visited in England. Most of all it was a fulfillment of the vision Bonhoeffer had first begun to develop even in his doctoral dissertation, "The Communion of Saints." The idea that we know God not in isolation but in community was now being demonstrated. Daily meditation on Scripture, prayer, singing, even mutual confession to at least one other student, were built into the schedule, much to the surprise—and sometimes displeasure—of the students.

One of the greatest surprises for the students was Bonhoeffer's idea that confession is essential to the community. If our fellowship is to have any depth at all, it must include an acceptance and affirmation of each other that responds to the whole person, not just the select, public parts. As four-year-old Billy put it (in one of those innumerable internet lists of cute sayings), "When someone loves you, the way they say your name is different. You just know that your name is safe in their mouth." We're not safe if we are not fully known, if there are dark parts of our soul which we keep secret. Real love says: I see you, I know you, I love you.

An important observation for evangelicals is that Bonhoeffer did not dispense with academics in favor of a more devotional or a more practical approach to pastoral training. Serious biblical and theological study was very much a part of the life of the seminarians. We evangelicals seem less and less interested in or even approving of academic work by our pastors. As one church "expert" put the matter at a pastors' conference as far back as 1989, "We've got to stop training our pastors to be scholars, stop drowning them in so much theology and Bible, and start concentrating on leadership development." What is the result when such thinking shapes the life of the church? Strong leaders with no idea where they are leading people.

Bonhoeffer kept matters in perfect balance, made somewhat easier by the fact that the school was a live-in situation, which was necessary if they were to be fully immersed in devotion, praxis, and biblical theology. Learning from this seminary example is difficult for our churches because we American Christians spend so little time together, far less in a month than Bonhoeffer's seminarians did in a day.

For those students, the greatest surprise was the devotional di-

The Seminary at Finkenwalde | 91

mension, the focus on spiritual formation. Bonhoeffer never let them forget that:

> There are three things for which the Christian needs a regular time alone during the day: meditation on the Scripture, prayer, and intercession. All three should find a place in the daily period of mediation (*DBWE* 5:86).

Raised in a culture in which the Bible, if noticed at all, was simply the object of academic and historical studies, the students were a bit irritated at first that Bonhoeffer expected them to hear Scripture as if it were an extended love letter from God to them personally. He would not bend on this matter, despite their early complaints, and expected them to have both private and shared times of prayer and Bible reading each day.

Samuel Wells, vicar of St. Martin-in-the-Fields in London, notes that:

> Bonhoeffer was rooted in an accountable community. He saw that for his Confessing Church to have any backbone, it needed to be led by pastors who took for granted the simple, straightforward practices of daily prayer, the confession of sin, the studying of scripture, and the sharing of communion.[3]

In many of our evangelical churches, watching videos of Bible teachers seems to have replaced much Bible study. I long ago discovered that if you want to study scholarly journals devoted exclusively to Scripture, you find few options available from an evangelical perspective. These journals are most often found in more progressive circles. The Bible, in and of itself, receives a far less careful study in evangelical circles than elsewhere. I suspect it has something to do with the evangelical sense that most of the answers to questions about the Bible were answered in the nineteenth century. More broadly, perhaps it is part of what Mark Noll pointed out some forty years ago when he said, "The scandal of the evangelical mind is that there is not much of an evangelical mind."

The Bible, of course, is not merely to be studied but to be heard personally and deeply. This requires time spent in meditation on the texts. One Confessing Church leader told Bonhoeffer, "We have no time for meditation now, the ordinands have to learn how to preach and catechize." Bonhoeffer wrote of this in a letter to Barth, saying,

"It seemed to me to reveal either a total incomprehension of what a young theologian today is like or a criminal ignorance of the real roots of preaching and catechesis" (*DBWE* 14:254). We cannot speak the word of God until we have heard it ourselves.

One of the first students to arrive at the seminary was Eberhard Bethge. Bonhoeffer quickly recognized in Bethge an unusual combination of scholarly aptitude and pastoral heart. When Bonhoeffer called upon the students to begin the practice of confession with one another, it was Bethge whom he asked to hear his confession. Bethge remained a deeply loyal friend until Bonhoeffer's death in 1945. In fact, his active loyalty to Bonhoeffer remained strong until his own death in 2000.

The seminary, which had settled in Finkenwalde in northern Germany, was declared illegal and was closed by the Nazis in September of 1937, two months after the opening of the concentration camp at Buchenwald. For another two years Bonhoeffer continued to mentor his students by visits and letters, though little came of his efforts. Many of the former students were imprisoned at one time or another but the larger portion of them were drafted into the army. A great many of them were killed in battle.

After the seminary's closing, Bonhoeffer traveled a great deal, though not often for pleasure. He attended conferences, met with a wide variety of individuals, and worked with former students throughout Germany. And he wrote. His pen was one of his primary tools in seeking to clarify his thoughts. His letters—more numerous than I have the patience to count!—were worth saving. That's why we have hundreds preserved in the volumes of his complete works.

He published two books during this period, each aimed at presenting a different aspect of the experience at Finkenwalde. The first, titled in English *The Cost of Discipleship*, was titled in German *Nachfolge*, which means simply "following" or "following after." For Bonhoeffer a disciple is a follower, not merely a believer. A disciple lives by the words of the master, not merely by words and doctrines about the master. At the heart of Bonhoeffer's thinking about Christ is his conviction that we are being called to follow a *living* Lord. A proper doctrine of Christ is fine but insufficient. We love Jesus, not just the idea of a Savior.

Discipleship

The theme of total devotion to the living Christ which had marked Bonhoeffer's lecture in Barcelona in December of 1928[4] became amplified in his thinking during the next few years. His friend, Jean Laserre, had helped him see that the Sermon on the Mount was actually a call to action, not merely an expression of lofty ideals. And Hitler's ferocious attempt to be the lord of the German people and to supplant Jesus Christ as the rightful Lord of all people, centered Bonhoeffer's mind all the more on his absolute and exclusive devotion to Christ alone.

Much of the life of Bonhoeffer's seminarians consisted in an extended study of the Sermon on the Mount. It was as if Bonhoeffer was still working through the whole new world view which Laserre had opened for him in helping him hear the call of the living Lord in that great Sermon. By the time the Gestapo closed Finkenwalde, his thoughts were already formed into a book.[5]

The preface of that book, *Discipleship*, begins with a great understatement. "In times of church renewal holy scripture naturally becomes richer in content for us" (*DBWE* 4:37). When the church is fighting for its life against the power of darkness, the Bible becomes absolutely crucial to our thinking and our spiritual lives. No one in 1937 would have missed that meaning. The Bible becomes "richer in content for us" just as water quenches the thirst and fulfills the man who has crawled for three days across a desert to reach the oasis.

Chapter One begins with the words etched into the hearts of Christians all over the world today:

> Cheap grace is the mortal enemy of our church. Our struggle today is for costly grace. . . . Cheap grace means grace as doctrine, as principle, as system. . . . Cheap grace means justification of sin but not of the sinner. . . . Cheap grace is grace without discipleship, grace without the cross, grace without the living, incarnate Jesus Christ" (*DBWE* 4:43f).

"Costly grace" demands single-minded devotion to Jesus Christ. His readers would have known that he meant this to contrast directly with most Germans' allegiance to Hitler. "It is the call of Jesus Christ which causes a disciple to leave his nets and follow him" (*DBWE* 4:45). To follow Jesus, of course, is to deny oneself and take up the cross. "It is costly," Bonhoeffer writes, "because it costs people their lives. . ." (*DBWE* 4:45).

Can you imagine a televangelist today teaching such an understanding of grace? This is not a message delivered by those who want to be popular. Nonetheless, there is no way to deny that this is the call of Jesus himself, finding expression in the words of Dietrich Bonhoeffer.

Bonhoeffer was fully aware of and grateful for Luther's discovery of the long-lost Gospel of grace: justification by faith. He never strayed from the conviction that grace on God's part and faith on ours are essential to life. He was also aware, however, that history had not been kind to Luther's great insight. He observed that "what emerged victorious from Reformation history was not Luther's recognition of pure, costly grace, but the alert religious instinct of human beings for the place where grace could be had the cheapest" (*DBWE* 4:49). The Good News is easy to abuse! Few would actually say what they nevertheless seem to believe, that it doesn't matter much what we do because God will forgive us anyway.

Cheap grace weakens not only the discipleship of the individual but, as a matter of course, it weakens the church. "Is the price that we are paying today with the collapse of the organized churches anything else but an inevitable consequence of grace acquired too cheaply?" (*DBWE* 4:53).

His criticism of the German churches fits our churches, too. "We poured out rivers of grace without end, but the call to rigorously follow Christ was seldom heard," says Bonhoeffer (*DBWE* 4:53f) as if he were speaking of us today. Our evangelism seems designed rather deliberately to broaden the narrow gate, to ease the rigors of the hard path, to create "saved Christians" who are not in fact followers of Jesus Christ.

One factor in modern evangelical churches' efforts to be "relevant" is the desire to address people at the point of their perceived needs. Are they lonely? Then we shape our message to emphasize Jesus as a cure for loneliness. Are they anxious? Then we speak to them about assurance. Such an approach is not inherently misguided, so long as it does not become the shaper of the Gospel we preach.

I recently saw a clip on YouTube in which an interviewer was talking with people in Scandinavia about their belief, or lack of belief, in God. One fellow ended the conversation quickly and simply by saying, "I don't need God." Since the Great Revival of the early eighteenth century and the Second Great Awakening in the first half of the nineteenth century, evangelists have sought to make people feel badly about themselves so that the evangelist could then relieve the pain with the Gospel. Evangelism centered on needs-fulfillment wouldn't have much to say to this man.

Bonhoeffer notices that when Jesus called someone to follow him, there was no word that the follower would become happier. Jesus says to Levi, "Follow me," and Levi gets up and follows. "The text," observes Bonhoeffer, "is not interested in psychological explanations for the faithful decisions of a person. Why not? Because there is only one good reason for the proximity of call and deed: *Jesus Christ himself*" (*DBWE* 4:57). Christ-centered evangelism will lead to Christ-centered Christians. Self-centered evangelism leads to self-centered "Christians."

"Only the believers obey," Bonhoeffer wrote, "and only the obedient believe" (*DBWE* 4:63). This, says Bethge, is the central theme of *Discipleship* (*DB* 450). We love Jesus as Savior but are dubious about Jesus as Lord. We cannot think, then, that Bonhoeffer would fit well into a modern American evangelical setting. He would be horrified. The lessons learned at such great cost for the Christians in Germany are utterly lost on us.

Ironically, Bonhoeffer's *Discipleship* is well known and often read in evangelical circles. We cheer for him in his great call for devotion to Jesus Christ but we do not actually pay much attention. This is not a new problem. Jesus himself knew there would be those who call him "Lord, Lord" but do not live by the things he said (Luke 6:46).

Bonhoeffer knows that we humans like to cover our sins with a pretended inability to understand exactly what God is asking of us. We try to use uncertainty as a smokescreen to excuse our disobedience. Bonhoeffer sees through the pretense and knows its origin:

> The serpent in paradise put this conflict into the heart of the first human "Did God say?" People are torn away from the clear commandment and from simple childlike obedience by ethical doubt, by asserting that the commandment still needs interpretation and explanation. "Did God say?" People are made to decide by the power of their own knowledge of good and evil, by the power of their conscience to know what is good. The command-

ment is ambiguous [we claim]; God intends for people to interpret it and decide about it freely. Even thinking this way is already a refusal to obey the commandment (*DBWE* 4:71).

A desire to continue in sin is not the only reason people seek ways to excuse themselves from simple obedience. We also tend to cower in fear, dreading the thought that God may demand everything from us. He may lead us into suffering. The fear is realistic; God's way may very well include suffering. It certainly includes self-sacrifice, the perfect symbol of which is the Cross of Jesus Christ. When we walk his path, we walk the path of the cross. We must understand, though, that:

> The cross is neither misfortune nor harsh fate. Instead, it is that suffering which comes from our allegiance to Jesus Christ alone. The cross is not random suffering but necessary suffering. . . . The cross is not the terrible end of a pious, happy life. Instead, it stands at the beginning of community with Jesus Christ. Whenever Christ calls us, his call leads us to death. (*DBWE* 4:86f).

Death, of course, is not the end but the beginning of life, of that new life shared with Jesus Christ. "For if we have been united with him in a death like his," says Paul, "we will certainly be united with him in a resurrection like his" (Romans 6:5). Bonhoeffer did not hear such words as merely pleasant religious sentiments. Among his last words were, "This is the end—for me the beginning of life" (*DB* 927).

If the central marks of that new life in Christ are love and grace, we will see those qualities in the followers of Christ. But love and grace are costly. It cost Jesus his life to forgive us. Just so, we must bear the cost of forgiving our brothers and sisters. This is *essential* to the Christian life, not optional. Only by forgiveness do we walk in fellowship with one another in the Spirit of Christ:

> The burden of a sister or brother, which I have to bear, is not only his or her external fate, manner, and temperament; rather, it is in the deepest sense his or her sin. I cannot bear it except by forgiving it, by the power of Christ's cross, which I have come to share. In this way Jesus' call to bear the cross places all who follow him in

the community of forgiveness of sins. Forgiving sins is the Christ-suffering required of his disciples. It is required of all *Christians.* (*DBWE* 4:88).

Forgiveness frees us to set aside the fig leaves we grabbed long ago in the garden. It frees us to step out from behind the bushes and stand simply before God, saying with both humility and boldness, "Here am I." Without forgiveness there will always be a barrier between us and God and a distance between brothers and sisters in Christ.

Forgiving another is costly. We must absorb the sin and its consequences. To forgive a debt is to say to the other, "You owe me nothing." In the process we lose whatever has been owed us. To forgive a sin against us is to forego any claim to revenge or even restitution as a basis of forgiveness.

"The cup of suffering will pass from Jesus," notes Bonhoeffer, "but *only by his drinking it*" (*DBWE* 4:90).We pay the price for the sin of the other, not instead of having Jesus pay it but as part of that divine payment. "I am now rejoicing in my sufferings for your sake, and in my flesh I am completing what is lacking in Christ's afflictions for the sake of his body, that is, the church" (Colossians 1:26).

The emphasis upon salvation by substitutionary atonement fails to capture the depth of the meaning of the cross. "We were united with Christ in a death like his," said Paul, and "We shall certainly be united with him in a resurrection like his" (Romans 6:5). It is not that Jesus died on the cross *instead* of us but that we are united with him on that cross. That's why we have to take up our cross. We walk Jesus' path all the way to Calvary. We suffer and die and live with Christ and in Christ. This understanding that we share in the suffering of Jesus Christ, says Bethge, is "the most profound idea ever expressed by Bonhoeffer" (*DB* 456).

There are two levels of forgiveness because there are two levels of offense. Bonhoeffer does not articulate them but seems to assume them. At the first level trust is not broken, relationships are essentially unaffected by minor offenses; i.e. the spilled glass of milk, the driver who might cut us off, the neighbor who cuts his lawn too early in the morning. In this case we say to the one who has offended us, "I am not angry and I seek no retribution." All that is required is graciousness on the part of the one offended. The second level is deeper because it is a response to a deeper, more hurtful offense. Dignity has been trampled, respect has been discarded and relationships have been broken. At this level there has been a breach of trust leaving the one who has been hurt a deep cost in offering forgiveness. The one who has been offended may offer forgiveness and find no response. There may be a certain healing in this and they remain ready to forgive, but it remains incomplete. On the other hand, for a relationship to be made whole again, a *metanoia* on the part of the offender needs to occur–a complete repentance and change of heart–in which it may be possible for a relationship to be restored, for the words "I trust you again" to be spoken.

Is such a deep level of forgiveness possible? Of course. God does that with us all the time. Having received such abundant forgiveness, have we none to share? Did Jesus not warn us that those who withhold forgiveness are not forgiven? (Matthew 6:14-15).

Costly forgiveness, of course, is not the only burden that is to be borne by the follower of Christ. Just as the cross was not the first and sole sacrifice made by Jesus, we who walk his path will experience hard times, painful losses, broken relationships.

In words that he will later echo in *Life Together*, Bonhoeffer speaks of Christ as the mediator. We are accustomed to think of Christ as the mediator between us and God, but Bonhoeffer expands this thought to include our mediated relationships with one another and with all the world. We are not directly connected to one another, even in—or especially in—our Christian fellowship. We meet one another always and only *in Christ*. "*He is the mediator*, not only between God and human persons, but also between person and person, and between person and reality" (*DBWE* 4:94).

In a very real sense, then, all ministry is bridge building. We seek to build bridges between people and their Lord, between people and God's Word, and simply between people. The key to such relational bridge building is usually little more than helping people learn to be listeners, to hear God, to hear God's Word, to hear one another.

The romantics among us like to imagine such perfect communion between people that we can know each other immediately, without intervention or barrier between us. This is merely self-deception, a self-imposed illusion. "The illusion is immediacy. It has blocked faith and obedience" (*DBWE* 4:94f). Since we are who we are only in our communion *with Jesus Christ*, we can meet one another only *in Jesus Christ*. To think otherwise is to pretend we are not dependent upon Christ in this area of our lives and hearts. It is, therefore, to block faith and obedience.

We are, in fact, alone with Christ. "Christ intends to make the human being lonely. As individuals they should see nothing except him who called them" (*DBWE* 4:92). These words may seem almost threatening to us. They create some degree of a double fear within us. First, we are afraid to be face to face with Christ. Surely his face will show how disappointed he is in us. That's why so much of our prayer life is a matter of telling God what we want him to do for us and then quickly getting up and walking away without awaiting a response.

Henri Nouwen understood that Christ shares his loneliness with us and he understood that we have not the power to banish loneliness from the heart of another:

> The minister who has come to terms with his own loneliness and is at home in his own house is a host who offers hospitality to his guests. . . . The paradox indeed is that hospitality asks for the creation of an empty space where the guest can find his own soul. Why is this a healing ministry? It is healing because it takes away the false illusion that wholeness can be given by one to another.[6]

Second, we are afraid to let go of whatever connections we may already feel with others. However imperfect those connections may be, at least they help us and at least they are known, whereas contemplating a direct communion with Jesus Christ is like stepping into a dark unknown. We read of the mystics and their "dark night of the soul" and fear the darkness. No wonder we struggle so much with Jesus' seemingly harsh words: "Whoever comes to me and does not hate father and mother, wife and children, brothers and sisters, yes, and even life itself, cannot be my disciple" (Luke 14:26).

Such thoughts and fears are devilish illusions, shattered by the experience of anyone and everyone who has dared to be open to the Spirit of Jesus Christ. Not only is communion with him deep, rich, sweet, but it also binds us more closely in love to others. As Christ's love fills our hearts, we love our brothers and sisters all the more deeply. It is Christ's love which most truly binds us together.

As those whose entire being has been claimed in totality by Jesus Christ, we receive any form of communion with others as a gift, not as our right and not as something within our ability to create. Such communion is always and only a part of our oneness with Christ himself. "Anything not given me through Christ, the incarnate one, was not given to me by God," writes Bonhoeffer. "Anything not given me for the sake of Christ does not come from God."[7]

We see here—as is so common in Bonhoeffer—a staunch rejection of any form of idolatry. There is no competition for Jesus in our hearts, in our love, in our lives.

With these strong and challenging thoughts, Bonhoeffer concludes the first five chapters of the book *Discipleship*, having expanded with great care the theme he first announced in Barcelona in 1929: devotion to Jesus Christ is to be all-consuming. Chapter Six is an extended exposition of the Sermon on the Mount and the remaining chapters spell out practical implications of what he has learned from this message of Jesus.

The themes of *Discipleship* were seen as alarming to those who were trying to bring Christianity into line with Nazism. One of the foremost Luther scholars of the time was the German theologian Paul Althaus, who wrote, ". . . we cannot stand by idly and let the new Christian radicalism, by invoking the name of Jesus and the Sermon on the Mount, confuse the conscience of Christians with regard to law, nation government, and military service." That would be a laughable line—as if he had said we mustn't let Jesus and his teachings muddle our fine German Christianity—were it not for the seriousness of the situation. Althaus and so many other intellectual "leaders" had surrendered quickly and easily to Hitler, with tragic results.[8]

For very different reasons, Bonhoeffer himself came to see *Discipleship* as a dangerous book. In a letter written July 21, 1944, the day after the last failed attempt on Hitler's life, Bonhoeffer wrote to his friend Bethge a letter which suggests that he had heard the reports of the failed assassination attempt of which he had been a part. Looking back on his life and looking forward to an almost certainly doomed future, he wrote "May God lead us kindly through these times, but above all, may God lead us to himself" (*DBWE* 8:486).

He also wrote:

> I thought I myself could learn to have faith by trying to live something like a saintly life. I suppose I wrote Discipleship at the end of this path. Today I clearly see the dangers of that book, though I still stand by it (*DBWE* 8:486).

Today, especially among evangelicals, *Discipleship* is the most popular of Bonhoeffer's books. I wonder how many ponder this later idea that the book is dangerous. He didn't explain what danger he had in mind, so we'll never know for certain but there are some hints we can piece together.

Our first clue about the nature of the "danger" of *Discipleship* has to come from that 1944 letter itself. If the book is an expression of his desire to live a saintly life, then we need to know what could possibly be dangerous about such a desire. A life in which one tries to make oneself into a saint or even merely a "good Christian" is a life that remains self-centered. Like Peter in his brief attempt to walk on water, taking our eyes off Jesus causes us to be overwhelmed and to sink before we reach Jesus. It is clear in *Discipleship* that Bonhoeffer wants very much to be Christ-centered but it is not so clear that he had yet learned how to move beyond trying to make something of himself.

The book can be dangerous, then, if it is read as an encouragement to try harder to make ourselves into good Christians. In that sense, it represents an immature Christian faith.

When we begin to understand that there is no such thing as a "self-made Christian" and begin to rid ourselves of all efforts to make ourselves into something, we find that we have to shed layer after layer of effort. We cannot make ourselves ethical beings. We cannot make ourselves loving or spiritual or even sacrificial. We are reduced to the stage Peter reached when the cock crowed for a second time: He broke down and wept (Mark 14:72). When there is nothing left of our good intentions but helpless tears, then we are beginning our new life in Jesus Christ. These, I think, are words which Bonhoeffer could have added to *Nachfolge* in 1944.

I have observed that there are three stages of Christian maturing, especially noticeable in new believers. At first, they are thrilled with the new sense of being known, forgiven, and loved by God. They want to devote every ounce of energy into serving God. They try hard to live *for God*. When they become exhausted and discouraged by the seeming impossibility of being perfect for God, they either abandon the faith or move to the second stage.

At this point come the words of grace that God is our sustainer. One learns that the single set of footprints in the sand are those of Jesus as he carries us. Then there is a time of great joy as they learn to receive life *from God*. Those who have learned this lesson are a delight to be around as they live with hearts filled with gratitude.

Finally, often without the person realizing what is happening, there is another kind of transformation. As one grows in godly wisdom and Christlikeness of character, one develops what John Matthews calls "responsible interdependence,"[9] not leaving behind the first two levels of faith but now living not just for God and not just from God, but *with God*.

With this overly simplified scheme in mind, we can say that *Discipleship* could easily be read as an encouragement to work hard at the first and most immature level of Christian living, in which we try to make ourselves into saints. The book, in other words, could be seen as merely an expression of idealism.

There are other clues in Bonhoeffer which suggest an even deeper danger. John de Gruchy in his introduction to the *Letters and Papers*, notes a crucial theme that emerges only in Bonhoeffer's later writings. De Gruchy says that,

> Whereas in Discipleship the emphasis was on the "church against the world," a church with clear-cut boundaries, in his Ethics the boundaries became more open, preparing the way for his conclusion that just as Christ is the "human being for others," so the church "exists only for others" (*DBWE* 8:27).

As we have seen, the early years of the Confessing Church and the resistance against Hitler tended to focus too much on protesting against Nazi interference only in the life of the church. It was as if the church were seen as being threatened by the evil world and needing to be guarded against it. When Bonhoeffer wrote *Ethics* and the letters from prison, one of his new concerns was not to protect the church *from* the world but to send the church *into* the world. He had learned to value not sainthood but servanthood and he had learned that the proper context for Christian discipleship is not the church but the world.

Life Together

After *Discipleship*, Bonhoeffer wanted to share with the church what life had been like in his communal experiment at Finkenwalde. The book *Life Together*, written mostly in September of 1938, describes the ways in which Bonhoeffer shaped the school and why he did it that way. In the process, he seems to have hoped he would be teaching about the core of the life of a congregation, no matter what outward form it might take.

Even in writing what could have been merely a mundane description of a temporary school, Bonhoeffer remains as always a theologian and teacher. "His thought resonates," says Wayne Whitson Floyd, Jr., "with a prescience, subtlety, and maturity that continually belies the youth of the thinker" (*DBWE* 5:vii).

Officially, Finkenwalde was a school and as such there were high academic standards. More than just an academic institution, however, Finkenwalde was molded in a monastic image. The men lived and studied and ate together as a community. They prayed together, listened to the reading of the Bible together, even had private time for meditation and prayer at the same time each day. These disciplines formed what Geffrey Kelly calls the "sustaining structures" of the seminary at Finkenwalde (*DBWE* 5:3).

What practical lessons for a congregation could possibly come from such a unique situation?

First, a warning: monastic seclusion is good only for a time. "Jesus Christ lived in the midst of his enemies," Bonhoeffer warns us. "So Christians, too, belong not in the seclusion of a cloistered life but in the midst of enemies. There they find their mission, their work" (*DBWE* 5:27). We are sent into the world, just as Jesus himself was sent into the world (John 17:18). Time together is necessary, however, because like all families we need bonding time as a foundation for service outside the family. One does not supplant the other.

We cannot simply gather all the members of a congregation together for half a year, as at Finkewalde, or even a weekend, but we can provide regular weekend or even week-long retreats for smaller groups. Such retreats need Bible study, prayer, and personal sharing in one form or another. Weekly small groups for prayer and Bible study can also foster a strong sense of community.

Second, we are united with one another and with God only *in Christ*. If we are to seek a relationship with Christ, we seek relationships within the community of Christ's people, not exclusively through individual relationships. Bonhoeffer, though expressing his views perhaps too strongly remained convinced that we meet Christ only in the community of God's people; we are never to seek a direct person to person relationship. All relationships are a form of Christian fellowship.

> Christian community means community through Jesus Christ and in Jesus Christ. There is no Christian community that is more than this, and none that is less that this . . . . What does that mean? It means, first, that a Christian needs others for the sake of Jesus Christ. It means, second, that a Christian comes to others only through Jesus Christ. It means, third, that from eternity we have been chosen in Jesus Christ, accepted in time, and united for eternity (*DBWE* 5:31).

Bonhoeffer took very seriously Paul's image of the church as the body of Christ (e.g., 1 Corinthians 12:27), as well as the image of us as agents of reconciliation.

> So if anyone is in Christ, there is a new creation: everything old has passed away; see, everything has become new! All this is from God, who reconciled us to himself through Christ, and has given us the ministry of reconciliation; that is, in Christ God was reconciling the world to himself, not counting their trespasses against them, and entrusting the message of reconciliation to us. So we are ambassadors for Christ, since God is making his appeal through us; we entreat you on behalf of Christ, be reconciled to God. For our sake he made him to be sin who knew no sin, so that in him we might become the righteousness of God (2 Corinthians 5:17-21).

We have usually seen this passage as an encouragement to become reconciled with God, as if it were a once-for-all event, but Bonhoeffer sees that we are in continual need of being reconciled and that we, as the body of Christ, are to be conveying grace and speaking God's word for one another. "We are insufficient for our own salvation or for speaking God's word to ourselves," he says, since "these are *extra nos* [outside us] and are communicated—mediated?—through others" (*DBWE* 5:31).

One of Jesus' parables expresses very perfectly this dimension of the life of the church. Four friends brought to Jesus a paralytic. Too weak to come to Jesus himself, the man—just like us—needed to be carried to Jesus by his brothers in faith. Strikingly, the text says that when Jesus saw *their* faith, he healed the man and forgave him all his sins (Mark 2:3-12).

We can and must believe *for* one another. In fact, we can believe more strongly for one another than we can for ourselves. This is not a sign of some flaw in us. It is simply the way we are created, to be a community of interdependent children of God.

> Therefore, Christians need other Christians who speak God's Word to them . . . the Christ in their own hearts is weaker than the Christ in the word of other Christians. Their hearts are uncertain; those of their brothers and sisters are sure (*DBWE* 5:32).

Third practical lesson for the congregation is that one of the greatest enemies of the Christian is the idealist. The one who measures the quality of the fellowship by some lofty ideal is failing to accept the reality which God is creating in our midst. Our fellowship, remember, is built on who we are *in Christ*, not by how ideally we measure up as Christians. The idealist, in fact, will end up as the judge of the fellowship, as the one who brings condemnation where Christ is bringing grace (*DBWE* 5:34). Montaigne once remarked that, "In trying to make themselves angels, men transform themselves into beasts."[10]

Those who begin a new fellowship of persons united around a single ideal, of course, are in grave danger of slipping into condemning others if the vision fails or, at the least, of rejecting others who do not share the ideal. That is often why they must begin new churches. Established congregations are too difficult to unite around new ideals. Is ambition in God's work just another form of idealism? Perhaps so.

One of the unique features of Finkenwalde was that, because of its small size, one person—Bonhoeffer himself—could be president, dean, faculty, and chaplain all at once. The two dozen students discovered that their multi-gifted teacher was even happy to mentor each of them. "Those students who were meeting him for the first time," wrote Bethge, reflecting of course on his own first meeting with Bonhoeffer, "remarked on the surprising and intense readiness of their seminary director to make himself available to them" (*DB* 419).

Mentoring is extremely valuable but time-consuming and therefore is seldom a part of pastoral ministry in our churches today. It was central to the ministry of Jesus with the Twelve but, of course, he never built big churches like those we aspire to in our day. He mentored twelve men for three years, had one fail him completely, and established no institution. All he did was change Western civilization through twelve—well, eleven—thoroughly mentored fishermen and tax collectors.

Bonhoeffer then went on to describe some of the specific forms of fellowship experienced by the students and the importance of time spent alone.

The day with others begins with communal worship. "For Christians," Bonhoeffer says, "the beginning of the day should not be burdened and haunted by the various kinds of concerns they face during the working day. The Lord stands above the new day, for God has made it" (*DBWE* 5:51).

Most important during this time is the ancient church practice of praying the Psalms together. The book of Psalms is a schoolbook of prayer and in particular the schoolbook of Jesus' prayer.[11] Though he will later come to value the Old Testament on its own terms, at this point Bonhoeffer still reads it in very strictly Christological terms.[12] The Psalms, accordingly, he sees as being the book of Jesus' prayers (*DBWE* 5:55). When the Psalmist speaks of his own innocence, we are to hear Jesus professing innocence. We in turn are to adopt the prayers as our own, never forgetting that we are joining Christ in *his* prayers.

To call the Psalms a school of prayer means that we learn from them how to pray for ourselves. We learn to pray the Word of God. After all, isn't the promise that our prayer will be answered when we pray in harmony with his will? "And this is the boldness we have in him, that if we ask anything according to his will, he hears us. And if we know that he hears us in whatever we ask, we know that we have obtained the requests made of him" (1 John 5:14-15). By praying the Psalms we learn to pray from his perspective.

Is this the meaning of praying "in his name"? Our prayer is really *his* prayer. Such praying does not come naturally for us but must be learned by persistent discipline, which a regular praying of the Psalms provides for us.

As we learn to pray Jesus' prayer, we will be less and less inclined to pray in self-centered ways. Having led a great many prayer meetings over the years, I have long since learned that nearly always the first and most numerous requests are related to physical health. A few are related to marriage and a few to work. Rarely does anyone ask for prayer on behalf of the church or of the Kingdom. Almost never are there requests for spiritual growth. Praying the Psalms will help us get our minds off ourselves and help us to begin seeing and praying from God's perspective.

The praying of Psalms "teaches us to pray as a community" (*DBWE* 5:57). The Psalms were not written for private devotion but for public worship, though of course they are wonderfully used in both ways.[13] They raise us out of ourselves to pray as responsible members of the body of believers. Prayer, he wrote, "is not a matter of a unique pouring out of the human heart in need or joy, but an unbroken, indeed continuous, process of learning, appropriating and impressing God's will in Jesus Christ on the mind" (*DBWE* 5:57f).

Praying a Psalm together at Finkenwalde was followed by a hymn, after which the attention of the community was turned to Scripture reading. Bonhoeffer was a lifelong reader of the *Losungen*, the daily text and prayer published by the Moravian Brethren and others were users of a similar devotional called "Bread for Today." He warned the students, however, that the "Holy Scriptures are more than selected Bible passages, It is also more than 'Bread for Today'" (*DBWE* 5:59). The Bible must be read and heard in large passages and whole books, because the Scriptures "do not consist of individual sayings, but are a whole and can be used most effectively as such."

Was it Clint Eastwood who first used the line, "Works for me"? That may reflect a certain strong American pragmatism, but it makes for a very bad approach to the Bible. "It is far more important for us to know what God did to Israel, in God's son Jesus Christ, than to discover what God intends for us today" (*DBWE* 5:62). *We are to find our place in God's Kingdom rather than find God's place in our own lives.*

We share Psalms, study God's Word, and then we sing, said Bonhoeffer. We are to "be filled with the Spirit, as you sing psalms and hymns and spiritual songs among yourselves" (Ephesians 5:19). Literally, we are to *speak* psalms and hymns and songs. Paul doesn't mean we are to skip the music, just that the importance is on the message that is conveyed when we sing. Bonhoeffer is perhaps a bit more radical than most of us when he insists that

> The essence of all congregational singing on this earth is the purity of unison singing—untouched by the unrelated motives of musical excess—the clarity unclouded by the dark desire to lend musicality an autonomy of its own apart from the words (*DBWE* 5:67).

Throughout his writings, Bonhoeffer refers to hymns again and again. They seem to have contributed nearly as much to his spiritual formation as Scripture itself, but only because the good hymns embody and express the biblical message.

As I am writing these words, I am listening to Elīna Garanča sing the *Ave Maria* by William Gomez. I am not devoted to Mary, do not understand the language of the song, and cannot imagine a congregation ever singing such a difficult piece, but I hear the piece as music of deep devotion to God and it expresses my own devotion better than I ever can. Such music can be a wonderful expression of faith in and love for God but it has no place in the singing of the congregation, which must be simple enough that our first priority is not on getting the notes right but on hearing the Word aright.

Just as we hear and pray the Psalms as the prayers of the church, or more precisely as the prayers of Jesus Christ, so we pray with one voice, the one voice of the church. It is in our agreement, our unity, that our prayer has its deepest meaning, not in the outpouring of the heart of an individual. "If two of you agree about anything you ask for, it will be done for you by my Father in heaven" (Matthew 18:19).

The communal prayer at Finkenwalde may strike us as a bit odd. Bonhoeffer was so afraid that spoken prayer could become a mere expression of one's personality or even pride that he said only one person should pray on behalf of the whole community and that the same person should do all the praying for a period of weeks at a time. What if that person just doesn't feel like it on some particular day?

> From time to time a problem will arise where the person given the job of offering prayer for the community feels inwardly unable to offer prayer and would prefer to turn

> over the task to someone else for the day. However, that is not advisable. Otherwise, the community's prayers will be too easily controlled by moods that have nothing to do with life in the spirit (*DBWE* 5:70).

We've seen enough now to recognize a thread running through Bonhoeffer's thinking, a thread that will remain visible to the very end. We are followers of the living, present Jesus Christ, walking his path, praying his prayers. We are not walking our own path and expecting him to bless us as we go our way. This must surely be one of those lessons we are most in need of learning and most inclined to neglect. Time and again we treat our Lord as if he were some sort of requisition clerk, waiting for us to ask for something so that he'll know what to do for us and what to give us. Self-centered prayer, which consists solely of asking God to do things for us, must never become the greater part of our prayer life.

Psalms, songs, Scripture, prayer; all these lead us to a deep concluding worship in the sharing of Communion. The breaking of bread together is always shaped by the lesson learned long ago by the travelers to Emmaus, who discovered that in the breaking of bread with the risen Jesus, whom they had not recognized, "their eyes were opened, and they recognized him" (Luke 24:31).

For us the Communion service easily and commonly becomes merely a religious habit. As the climax of Word, song, and prayer, however, it can be much more: a revelation of Jesus Christ. "Examine yourselves," said Paul, "and only then eat of the bread and drink of the cup. For all who eat and drink without discerning the body, eat and drink judgment against themselves" (1 Corinthians 11:28-29). We are perhaps to discern the body in a double sense: We perceive Jesus as did the Emmaus travelers and we perceive that we together are the body of Christ.

In this way, the sharing of Communion becomes that moment in which God answers our prayer, "give us this day our daily bread." Communion with Jesus Christ and with one another, is this not the richest bread we could imagine?

Only now do we turn outward and go our ways unto work, whatever that may be on any given day. In a very real sense, our work becomes just an extension of our prayer and our worship. An old missionary once said we are to pray as if everything depends upon

God and work as if everything depends upon us. I think Bonhoeffer would have liked that. It helps us to see that our prayer and our work need one another. "Praying and working are two different things," said Bonhoeffer. "Prayer should not be hindered by work, but neither should work be hindered by prayer" (*DBWE* 5:74).

Work is not merely that which we must do in order to put food on our plates. Work "is only an instrument in the hand of God for the purification of Christians from all self-absorption and selfishness" (*DBWE* 5:75). Work puts us into a world where the danger of self-centeredness is minimized simply because there is work to be done, whether we like it or not at any given moment. In our work we begin to learn what Paul meant when he taught us to "pray without ceasing." Our work becomes our way of giving ourselves to something beyond ourselves:

> Thus every word, every deed, every piece of work of the Christian becomes a prayer, not in the unreal sense of being constantly distracted from the task that must be done, but in a real breakthrough from the hard It [the objectivity of our tasks] to the gracious You [the Lord himself] (*DBWE* 5:76).

In our work we are learning to pray with our hands as well as our hearts. Just as we are to pray in the name of Jesus, so "whatever you do, in word or deed, do everything in the name of the Lord Jesus" (Colossians 3:17).

Having completed the work to which the Lord has called us for the day—and not feeling guilty for the work not yet done—we come together again, this time for a meal. We remind ourselves that we worked, not for money but simply because God calls us to work. Our meals are not the fruit of our earnings but are a sign of God's grace. "It is God who must feed us," Bonhoeffer writes (*DBWE* 5:77). This reminder will help protect us from relegating God's grace to those areas of our lives where we feel a need for something more than we can take care of ourselves.

Finally, we come together at the end of the day, this time especially for intercessory prayer. We pray for our brothers and sisters and for those in the world beyond our community. We end our prayer asking God's protection during the night. We will sleep well when we begin to see sleep as a great act of faith. We are letting ourselves be unprotected, unless God is our guardian. "Now I lay me down to sleep; I pray the Lord my soul to keep." That was once not just a cute little children's verse but a real prayer, as it ought to be for us even this very day.

Eugene Peterson likes to remind us that our Jewish forefathers understood the rhythm of the days somewhat differently than we do. The day began at sunset. It began, therefore, with a family meal and the great act of faith called sleep.[14] Then, with the day half done, the work of the hands would begin.

One interesting application of this understanding of sleep as an expression of faith is found in Richard Foster's excellent book, *The Celebration of Discipline*. New to the world of spiritual discipline and spiritual formation? One way to begin, says Foster, is to close the day by entrusting your dream life to the Spirit of Jesus Christ, the Lord of night as well as day.[15] "Yours is the day," quotes Bonhoeffer from Psalm 74, "yours also the night" (*DBWE* 5:80).

The day alone next occupies Bonhoeffer's attention. We may protest that he has already filled our day from morning to evening. When have we time alone? Bonhoeffer always found time or made time. Admittedly, he was extraordinary. Bethge comments that he could accomplish in two or three hours what would be a whole day's work for others (*DB* 429). Yet, as he guided the daily routines of the students, they discovered that they, too, had time alone amidst all the busyness of the day.

The single most common reason given in our churches today for people not taking part in the whole life of the church is that they are simply too busy. As a young pastor, I sometimes felt badly about the church adding various activities to the already busy lives of people. That concern did not last long, however, as I discovered that all these busy, busy people knew all the television shows and movies. I began to realize that busyness was not the problem at all. Rather, they were a people having to use large portions of their day to unwind from the stresses of daily life. Had they been walking with the Lord, doing no more and no less than he called them to and entrusting their challenges to God, they would not have needed several hours each day "unwinding."

A good friend of mine, Dr. Ray Anderson of Fuller Seminary, told me once he never had a bad day. And he meant it! He began each day by affirming, "This is the day the Lord has made; I *will* rejoice and be glad in it." Whatever problems arose, Ray considered them the Lord's problems, not his. He was committed to this way of thinking. He was called to be faithful to the Savior, not to be the Savior who conquered all problems life might throw at him.

I always thought Ray was a good example but only occasionally did I remember to begin my day with that affirmation and to hold on to it all day long. And then I was diagnosed with cancer. That vow has been the center of my attitude from the beginning. The cancer is God's problem, not mine. To my surprise (I admit with some embarrassment) I've had a few very hard days but never a down day. Even the most discouraging days included a certain faith-borne optimism. Some days were physically hard but I simply accepted each day as it came. Thanks be to God.

Those who learn to live in that way choose not to be overcome by stress and are free to be attentive to the call of God day by day, hour by hour. They find that there is time for fellowship, time for work, and time to be alone.

Bonhoeffer recognized both that community and aloneness are needed, but that some people avoid one or the other for a variety of inadequate reasons. "Many persons seek community because they are afraid of loneliness," he observed (*DBWE* 5:81). They—we!—tend to seek company not so much out of love as out of a need to escape loneliness. "More often than not, they are disappointed," Bonhoeffer added (*DBWE* 5:81).

The lesson, then, can be summarized in two complementary ideas:

> Whoever cannot be alone should beware of community.
> . . . Whoever cannot stand being in community should beware of being alone (*DBWE* 5:82).

Finally, we cannot fail to notice that one of the most urgent questions for the followers of Christ has been neglected altogether, both in *Discipleship* and in *Life Together*. In fact, Bonhoeffer never answers the question: How do we know what Christ wants for us today? If we are to live not by rules or principles but by the will of God, we must have confidence that we truly know God's will.

Why would Bonhoeffer not respond to such an obvious and important question? Though he himself, so far as I know, never ex-

The Seminary at Finkenwalde | 113

plained the omission, I suspect it is because we cannot answer "How do we know the will of God?" without slipping right back into principles. There is no formula possible and, for those who are really following Jesus Christ, there is no formula needed. Faith means being entrusted to Christ, open to and present for the Spirit of God. A part of that trust is the confidence that the Lord is a Master Communicator who wants us to know his will and who is quite capable of conveying that will to us. Being immersed in Scripture and being in genuine communion with brothers and sisters in Christ will sharpen our sensitivity to the voice of the Lord, but ultimately it is simply faith which makes us good receivers of God's revelation of himself and of his will.

Discipleship and *Life Together* form a unit, each being incomplete without the other. The emphasis in the first is on the meaning of an individual's relationship with Jesus Christ. There are no "private" disciples, however. Jesus chose twelve to be together, not to give each one individual attention. So *Life Together* expands the view of the Christian life to include the broader and very essential dimension first exposited in *The Communion of Saints*: we *together* are the body of Christ. We are a fellowship of mutual disciplemakers.

Later we will see Bonhoeffer wrestling with a third, equally important dimension: the Church and the World. We are not Christians alone. Nor can we be obedient to our Lord if we are a ghetto, gathered together for protection against the world. Rather, as Bonhoeffer makes clear in *Ethics* and *Letters and Papers*, we follow Jesus Christ *through the experience of the Cross into the world*. We are each followers of Christ; we are together followers of Christ; and we are followers of Christ into the world.

Endnotes

1. Bethge writes that this principle was the most important expectation Bonhoeffer had for the ordinands at the Seminary at Finkenwalde (DB 428).
2. Karl Barth at first was critical of the school's monastic tendencies, though he later came to approve of the school.
3. Samuel Martin, "What Bonhoeffer Knew," *Christian Century*, July 22, 2015: 33.
4. "Jesus Christ and the Essence of Christianity," 1928, *DBWE* 10:342.
5. Glen Stassen points out that once he had written *Discipleship*, Bonhoeffer rarely mentioned the Sermon on the Mount. His work pushed him in other directions, though we may guess that, had his life not been cut short, there would have come a time when he would have drawn together all the themes that had occu-

pied his mind at various periods in his life. See Stassen, "Grace and Deliverance in the Sermon on the Mount," *Review and Expositor* 89, 1992: 232.

6   Henri Nouwen, *The Wounded Healer* (New York: Image Books, 1979).

7   *DBWE* 4:95f. Eugene Peterson makes a similar point when he says, "The grand essentials for me are immersion in Scripture and pursuit of prayer. We're not supposed to be dealing with the culture. We're supposed to be dealing with God." ("Return to the Timeless," *Leadership Journal*, Spring, 1993: 22).

8   The German editors' afterword to the German Edition of Bonhoeffer's Works, *DBWE* 4:290. See Robert P. Ericksen, *Theologians under Hitler*, for a thorough examination of three intellectuals who welcomed Hitler and became supportive of National Socialism.

9   John Matthews, *Anxious Souls Will Ask: The Christ-Centered Spirituality of Dietrich Bonhoeffer* (Wm. B. Eerdmans Publishing Co., 2005), 31. Matthews is encapsulating the ideas Bonhoeffer was seeking to express in some of his most powerful letters from prison.

10 Cited in Kenneth Clark, *Civilization* (New York: Harper & Row, 1969), 161.

11 The ideas about prayer found in *Life Together* are expanded in a smaller book Bonhoeffer wrote at about the same time: *The Prayerbook of the Bible*, bound with *Life Together* in *DBWE* 5. A helpful companion to this is the meticulous study, *Answering God*, by Eugene Peterson.

12 Andersen, Francis I., "Dietrich Bonhoeffer and the Old Testament," *Reformed Theological Review*, May-August, 1975: 40: "If we could extrapolate from *Creation And Fall* to the promise that began to emerge in *Letters and Papers from Prison*, we might speculate that Bonhoeffer's mature, Christocentric interpretation of the Old Testament would have become less explicit because typological interpretation is certainly `religious'. He would have now been more patient, not to say the last word (`Christ') too hastily. In his earlier work he could hardly reach this word quickly enough."

13 From prison on 15 May 1943, Bonhoeffer wrote to his parents: "I am reading the Bible straight through from the beginning and am just coming to Job, whom I especially love. I am also still reading the Psalms daily as I have done for years. There is no other book that I know and love as much. I am no longer able to read Pss. 3, 47, 70, and others without hearing them in the musical settings by Heinrich Schütz" (*DBWE* 8:81).

14 Eugene Peterson, *Answering God* (New York: HarperOne, 1991).

15 Richard Foster, *The Celebration of Discipline* (New York: HarperCollins, 1978, 1998).

CHAPTER FIVE

Conspiracy and Engagement

> *The source of a Christian ethic is not the reality of one's own self, not the reality of the world, nor is it the reality of norms and values. It is the reality of God that is revealed in Jesus Christ.*[1]

Disintegration of the Confessing Church

The Confessing Church for which Bonhoeffer had worked so hard was falling apart, piece by piece, person by person. The cost was too great for some. The danger was intimidating. The complexity of trying to form an alternate movement amidst chaotic conditions was overwhelming. And more and more pastors were being conscripted. Ultimately, most of Bonhoeffer's students lost their lives on Hitler's front lines.

It seems to have never occurred to anyone, including Bonhoeffer, that women could have provided good leadership while attracting far less attention from the Nazis.[2]

For several years after the closing of Finkenwalde and the other seminaries of the Confessing Church, attempts were made to find alternative ways to educate young men just entering their professional lives. Two alternatives were effective for a time but could not be sustained. The first was called the "collective pastorates" and the second was a series of circular letters written by Bonhoeffer to his former students and to the men in the collective pastorates.

Before we examine these two responses to the Gestapo's oppression, let's consider a lesson learned from the experience of the church in Germany. The experience of the Confessing Church, frankly, causes us to look with some alarm at our own situation in America and much of the West.

Most Christians in Germany considered the church to be irrelevant to a Christian life. They tended not only to ignore the church but one another as well. Many seemed to have accepted the Enlightenment view that faith is an essentially private affair and has no place in the public forum. Fellowship was simply not valued and "social justice" was simply not their business. When the crises came, one after another from the time of the First World War, Christians in Germany were totally unprepared. They knew neither how to create mutually supportive fellowships nor how to make a difference in the nation as a whole.

The Lutheran, Reformed, and Roman Catholic Churches functioned as state institutions, with pastors' salaries paid by the state. Without realizing it, they were being bought by the state. The problem was not just with the pastors. A strong cultural value in Germany was devotion to the authorities, so it was very difficult—impossible for many—to consider resisting that authority.

Sadly enough, even when the ascension of Hitler sparked the creation of the Confessing Church, that new church was dominated in its brief life by internal debates and self-interest. Having neglected in the early days their task to call the whole culture to accountability to God, they were quickly and thoroughly overwhelmed when the evil times demanded that they speak and act in strength, clarity of vision, and unity of action.

Paul's commendation of the Philippians, that they stood together firmly in the work of the Gospel and were never intimidated by their enemies (Philippians 1:27-28), could never have been spoken of the Christians and churches of Germany.

Ours is also a day of cultural upheaval. The church, which had grown accustomed to being the respectable cherry atop a pleasant sundae, has been set aside and left behind. Atheists now work harder at making converts than do Christians. We timidly allow our culture to silence us with a misconstrued argument that "separation of church and state" means Christians must not have a voice in public discourse.

Yet evangelicals, broadly defined, are so numerous that they represent a significant voting power. They tend to favor politicians who are most politically conservative. Those politicians may want a place for religion, not so much because they want Americans to be followers of Jesus Christ but because religion has a traditional place in the American story.

Unfortunately, that place has not always been honorable. Historically, conservative churches have been strong supporters of both racism and slavery. Permanently etched in my memory is a large photograph that appeared on the front page of the San Francisco *Examiner* during the civil rights struggles more than fifty years ago. The photo showed the deacons of a Baptist church in the South, standing before the doors of their church on a Sunday morning, locked arm in arm to prevent any Blacks from entering. The battle for equality and against racism is still prevalent today–even within our churches.

How can we fight to purge evil from our culture when we ourselves have been so deeply implicated in that evil ourselves?

Just as evil, though more subtle, is the popular view among many conservative Christians that they should not to be fighting for social justice because "social justice is just a code word for socialism." The devil must love that line! When Christians let a political stance keep them from valuing justice, they are serving the wrong lord.

The Collective Pastorates

Only sixty-seven seminarians were able to complete their theological education with Bonhoeffer in the two years after the closing of Finkenwalde. They were divided into two groups, assigned to one of two regions in northern Germany and given some mentoring by local Confessing pastors. Bonhoeffer joined them for covert meetings whenever he could. He himself was under increasing scrutiny by the Gestapo, which had forbidden him to teach in Germany. The seminarians had to be registered as associate pastors and their hidden meetings had to be very irregular.

It was really in his circular letters, which had to be passed off as personal letters, that Bonhoeffer was able to impart as much training as possible during those two years. From the very first of his letters, it is clear that one of the most pressing concerns for Bonhoeffer was the need simply to encourage those whose spirits, worn by the pressures and temptations, were lagging. In the very first letter, written shortly before Christmas of 1937, he wrote, "Years and generations pass away, but God's word does not. Indeed, we are merely one link in the chain." (*DBWE* 15:25). He knew that none of his young friends would want to be the weak link in the chain.

His second letter, written just a month later, acknowledges that the work of the Confessing pastors was exhausting and discouraging.

He reminds them that the real struggle is spiritual as they fight not against flesh and blood but all the forces of evil which seek to wrest the church from its rightful Lord. "So then," he says, "the struggle for the true church of Christ erupted. Or do you possibly believe that the devil would take such trouble to annihilate a small band of idealists who were carried away? No, the storm arose because Christ was in the boat" (*DBWE* 15:30). Not only is the battle spiritual, it is not even their battle anyway. It is warfare between Jesus Christ and evil. The young pastors are not to be taking the struggle personally.

Furthermore, they must recognize that, though their own weakness and sin may contribute to the difficulties, they must be careful not to slip into an accusatory kind of thinking. They are not to judge one another but support and encourage one another, reminding each other that the foundation is not one's own virtue but the word of God. That very word, when met with disobedience, seems a hard task-master. In our obedience, however, the word of God becomes "a gentle and light yoke" (*DBWE* 15:32).

Already in this second letter, we see that many of the young men were tempted to give in to the Nazi-dominated German Church. Hitler wanted the church to be pre-occupied with petty in-house matters so that it could continue to be irrelevant and harmless. That was actually beginning to sound pretty good to these young men. Bonhoeffer gave them a strong warning:

> Do you realize that with your step to the consistory, you give the struggle against the Confessing Church its most effective weapon? Is it clear to you that a Council of Brethren that would only practice a so-called spiritual leadership, as you wished, would be leading an illusory existence, which can be swept away in a moment? You yourself will be made responsible if the Confessing Church is crushed in this manner. Your step to the consistory is the strongest imaginable confirmation of the judgment of the anti-Christians against the Confessing Christians (*DBWE* 15:34)

It seems some were hoping to relieve the awful pressure by letting the church become "merely spiritual," that is, dealing only with faith, not with action. Let each individual decide what action he or she might take. It is not the business of the church to take social or civic action.[3]

By May 1939 Bonhoeffer must report that "several brothers have abandoned our cause" (*DBWE* 15:166). And in September, during Germany's invasion of Poland (starting World War II), the first of the brethren was killed in action. Bonhoeffer offered no easy comfort, saying simply that we "should not try to fill with human words those gaps that God has ripped open. They should remain open" (*DBWE* 15:273). And remain open they did, those and more wounds to come. For Bonhoeffer as for many others, the time of healing did not come on this side of the grave.

Travel to America and Back Again

The German people had let Bonhoeffer down. The ecumenical church had disappointed him. The Confessing Church was now quite impotent. Jesus Christ had not let him down. Bonhoeffer did not give up walking Christ's path, however lonely it had become.

So far, Bonhoeffer had not been drafted and did not know what he would do if it ever happened, except that he knew he would not fight against a supposed enemy which Germany had created for itself. He had once argued that fighting in defense of one's people, one's *volk*, was honorable.[4] That was clearly an irrelevant consideration now because Germany was the aggressor. Justice was not on the side of his country.

The Gestapo was finding more and more reasons to harass him, though not yet enough to arrest him. He knew that he was running out of options when friends from America offered a fresh alternative. They invited him to America to teach and lecture for an extended time. The purpose was simply to get Bonhoeffer out of Germany so they were scrambling to come up with specific plans.

The opportunity to escape to the United States came none too soon. On May 13, 1939, Bonhoeffer received the order to report for duty in the armed forces on May 22. He was granted an extension for a one-year trip to America and departed on June 2, after ominously handing to Bethge a copy of his will (*DB* 649).[5] After spending a few days in London with his sister Sabine and visiting Bishop George Bell, with whom he had a long friendship because of his earlier ecumenical work, Bonhoeffer arrived in New York on June 12. Twenty-four days later, he climbed aboard one of the last ships back to Germany.

Those were twenty-four days of great spiritual wrestling for Bonhoeffer. He had brought with him serious reservations about his "escape" from Germany. Even the day before the ship landed in New York, he wrote, "If only the doubts about my own path were overcome" (*DBWE* 15:219). The day after his arrival he wrote in his journal, "I do not understand why I am here, whether it was a sensible thing to do, whether the results will be worth while. . ." (*DBWE* 15:221).

The days were filled with visits, films, dinners in the homes of various people, worship services on Sunday mornings, and little snatches of reading and writing here and there. On June 20 he turned down the last of the options that had been offered him in the U.S. The question marks had become periods and exclamation points. His face was set again toward Germany. "What remains," he wrote, "are only the daily texts and intercessory prayers" (*DBWE* 15:229). Bonhoeffer knew that when all else is stripped away from us, Bible and prayer remain our daily foundations.

He had been finding particular relevance and power in the Moravian Daily Texts. Nearly every entry in his journal mentions the texts for the day. One was particularly haunting and personal for him: "Do your best to come before winter" (2 Timothy 4:21). These words of Paul to Timothy seemed to Bonhoeffer to be a call to return to Germany as soon as possible.

Sunday mornings were hard for him. Not only did worship make him long all the more for his brethren in Germany, but—with one exception—the sermons were awful. He was especially critical of a sermon at Riverside, which caused him to write, "Perhaps the Anglo-Saxons really are more religious than we, but they may not be more Christian, if they tolerate such sermons" (*DBWE* 15:224). The one exception, to his surprise, was by a Fundamentalist, who preached the Bible and preached the Gospel. He makes no mention of visiting the Abyssinian congregation and gives no reason why.

Finally, on July 8, he is aboard the ship, done with the American escape, and at peace while sailing into the storm. His last journal entry of the trip ends with these words:

> Since I have been aboard the ship, the internal tension about the future has stopped. I can think about the abbreviated time in America without reproach.—Daily Text: "It is good for me that I was humbled, so that I might learn your statutes" [Psalm 119:71]. One of my favorite sayings from my favorite psalm (*DBWE* 15:238).

Conspiracy Understood as Patriotism

Even before the American trip, Bonhoeffer had been aware of the conspiracy to assassinate Hitler, since his brother-in-law, Hans von Dohnanyi, was a key figure. Now, returning to Germany and eager to find his role in standing for the right and the good, he was invited into the inner circle of the conspirators. Dohnanyi arranged for him to have work in the Abwehr (military counter-intelligence), both to keep him out of the draft and to provide cover for his secretive missions. For a gentle-spirited pastor who loved his fatherland very deeply and who had long thought of himself as a pacifist, this must have seemed a step beyond anything he could have imagined.

Since his friendship with Jean Lasserre in America in 1930, Bonhoeffer had been strongly inclined toward pacifism. The decision to participate in an assassination attempt was exceedingly difficult for him. In the end, he felt he would bear part of the responsibility for all the deaths caused by Hitler if he did nothing to stop him. He did not declare himself innocent but simply did not see innocence as an available option. He believed that only the one who sees himself strictly and solely as an individual—not as part of the fabric of the human community—could evade feeling responsible for all that was happening because of Adolf Hitler.

More than six years earlier, we must remember, he had written that the church must be prepared to call the state to accountability, to bind the wounds of those victims by state injustice, and—in words whose outcome could not have been guessed at the time—"to seize the wheel [of state] itself" (*DBWE* 12:365).

It was time to jam the wheel.

Though potentially quite important, Bonhoeffer's role in the conspiracy turned out to be quite minor. The conspirators wanted to preserve Germany as much as possible, even while assassinating the Führer. Bonhoeffer's task was to build on his old ecumenical contacts to assure the Allies that Germany would surrender and a new, peace-seeking government would be in place as soon as Hitler was dead. They sought assurances from the West that a peace settlement could be established quickly so that Germany could immediately return to normal with no loss of sovereignty. No one—especially not Churchill—would give the idea a moment's thought. By now, they had no trust in the Germans. After all, hadn't Hitler been idolized?

Why should the people now be trusted? No, only total, unconditional surrender would do.

William Shirer suggests for us what seems to some a bit of an oddity in the thinking of the conspirators:

> One marvels at these German resistance leaders who were so insistent on getting a favorable peace settlement from the West and so hesitant in getting rid of Hitler until they had got it. One would have thought that if they considered Nazism to be such a monstrous evil as they constantly contended—no doubt sincerely—they would have concentrated on trying to overthrow it regardless of how the West might treat their new regime.[6]

Shirer has made an erroneous assumption here. While it is true that the conspirators did want to do whatever they could to insure Germany would remain free and sovereign after the death of Hitler, there is no evidence that they delayed their assassination plans while awaiting assurances from the West. They saw Hitler and the Nazis as mere aberrations and believed Germany would be fine once the Nazis were cleared away, if only the West would grant them freedom.

The conspirators moved ahead with several assassination attempts. On March 13, 1943, two small British-made bombs were hidden in a pair of wine bottles and smuggled aboard a plane with Hitler. The bombs failed to explode.

A week later, on March 21, a second attempt was made. Hitler was to tour a war factory in Berlin, where the conspirators had planted a suicide bomber, Colonel Rudolf von Gersdorff. The always unpredictable Hitler hurried through the plant, went nowhere near von Gersdorff, and was gone before the bomb was set to explode. Gersdorff barely had time to defuse it.

On the day of that second attempt, those conspirators who were in the extended Bonhoeffer family were gathered at the home of Rüdiger Schleicher, practicing a cantata to be performed at a birthday party for Bonhoeffer's father, Karl, the following week. There was not a single professional musician among them, but the high degree of artistry and musicianship in their family lent itself to occasions such as this. Bonhoeffer was playing the piano, Rudiger Schleicher and Emmi Delbruck Bonhoeffer the violins, Klaus Bonhoeffer the cello while the rest of the family, including Hans von Dohnanyi, made up the choir. And all in the midst of unbelievable tension.

While the Bonhoeffer's rehearsed in Berlin, they awaited news of Hitler's demise. The word never came. Meanwhile, Bonhoeffer was to report for military duty on Monday, March 22. Dohnanyi was able to have him deferred once again, not yet knowing that the entire military intelligence office was coming under the suspicious eye of the dreaded SS. On April 5 several arrests of conspirators were made, though the charges were only suspicions of illegal use of funds.

On July 20, 1944, in the final and most complicated attempt—portrayed in the film *Valkyrie*—a bomb nearly destroyed the room where Hitler was meeting with his generals. It, too, failed, and Hitler received only minor injuries. The bomb, hidden in a brief case, had been placed under a large table close to Hitler. Someone inadvertently kicked it and then moved it out of the way, behind the large, sturdy oak pillar supporting the table. That pillar was enough to divert the blast away from the Führer.[7]

Even so, in the confusion, the conspirators might have succeeded in taking over the government had they proceeded with enacting their plan. A new government was in place to take over immediately, however, the uncertainty of not knowing if Hitler was still alive caused some of the members to hesitate in fulfilling their roles. Order was restored, and Hitler's demand for immediate vengeance doomed the conspiracy.

Engagement to Maria

It was during the time of his work on *Ethics* and his early involvement with the conspiracy that Bonhoeffer began to realize that Maria von Wedemeyer, a young girl whom he had known for several years, was maturing into a remarkable young woman. In 1942, after a conversation with Maria and her grandmother, Ruth von Kleist, a strong supporter of Bonhoeffer's work, Dietrich found it hard to concentrate on his writing. His mind stayed with Maria.[8]

It was always difficult for Bonhoeffer to express his heart directly. Now, with this beautiful young woman calling forth his heart to his own surprise, he was quite awkward. In a letter in November of 1942 he asked her forgiveness for his clumsiness in saying what he was feeling. "I realize that words intended to say personal things come only with tremendous difficulty to me; this is a great burden for those around me" (*DBWE* 1:371). Whatever challenges he faced in putting his feelings into words, Maria seems to have had no trouble in reading his heart.

Maria's family[9] was concerned, not so much by the difference in their ages, eighteen years, but by the fact that Maria was simply so young and was still grieving the loss of her father and brother. They asked that Bonhoeffer not see or communicate with Maria for a full year. Bonhoeffer respected their concerns and so, with some difficulty, restrained himself. He never actually asked her to marry him, though each knew the matter was very much on the mind of the other.

Finally, having waited only three of the twelve months, 19-year-old Maria told her mother that it was time to take the next step. On January 13, 1943, she wrote to Bonhoeffer and said, "I'm now bold enough to write to you even though I've really no right whatever to answer a question which you have never asked me. With all my happy heart, I can now say yes."[10]

Those words must have been read by Bonhoeffer with a bittersweet mixture of joy and sorrow. The full happiness of love is bursting the bonds and overflowing their hearts, but the terrible situation in Germany in 1943 meant that Bonhoeffer and Maria would have almost no time together and never any time alone.

There is a story that has long circulated around the internet telling of a pastor some years ago giving a book to a dying patient in a Boston hospital. The book, *Heaven*, was written by Joe Bayley and included Bonhoeffer's January 1945 poem, "By Powers of Good." It is one of the very last words from Bonhoeffer's pen and was sent both to Maria von Wedemeyer and to his parents. Years later, the poem had been sent to Bayley by his son's fiancée, shortly after Joe's son had been killed in an accident.

By Powers of Good

> By faithful, quiet powers of good surrounded
> so wondrously consoled and sheltered here—
> I wish to live these days with you in spirit
> and with you enter into a new year.

The old year still would try our hearts to torment,
of evil times we still do bear the weight;
O Lord, do grant our souls, now terror-stricken,
salvation for which you did us create.

And should you offer us the cup of suffering,
though heavy, brimming full and bitter brand,
we'll thankfully accept it, never flinching,
from your good heart and your beloved hand.

But should you wish now once again to give us
the joys of this world and its glorious sun,
then we'll recall anew what past times brought us
and then our life belongs to you alone.

The candles you have brought into our darkness,
let them today be burning warm and bright,
and if it's possible, do reunite us!
We know your light is shining through the night.

When now the quiet deepens all around us,
O, let our ears that fullest sound amaze
of this, your world invisibly expanding
as all your children sing high hymns of praise.

By powers of good so wondrously protected,
we wait with confidence, befall what may.
God is with us at night and in the morning
and oh, most certainly on each new day.

The patient in the Boston hospital told the pastor both that she had found the book helpful and that her maiden name was Maria von Wedemeyer.

Endnotes

1   *DBWE* 5:49.

2   To pursue the theme of women in the German churches, see Susanne Hein, "The Public Witness of Women in the Confessing Church, 1934-1945," *On the Way*, Vol. 12, No. 2, Winter 1995-96. To examine Bonhoeffer's views more specifically, see Renate Bethge, "Bonhoeffer and the Role of Women," *Church and Society*, July/August 1995.

3   Persons advocating such a view were said to be "taking the inner line." Imprisoned and therefore inactive, Bonhoeffer later had to live as if he were taking such a line but he assured Bethge otherwise (Letter of 18 November 1943, *DBWE* 8:184).

4   *Basic Questions of a Christian Ethic*, 1929, *DBWE* 10:359.

5   From Tegel, Bonhoeffer also sent Bethge an informal will (23 November, 1943, *DBWE* 8:193).

6   William Shirer, *The Rise and Fall of the Third Reich* (New York: Simon and Schuster, 1960),1018.

7   Shirer, 1051-52.

8   Schlingensiepen, 298.

9   Meaning her mother and grandmother, since the war had already claimed the lives of Maria's father and brother.

10 *Love Letters from Cell 92*, 290.

CHAPTER SIX

Ethics

The question of good becomes the question of participating in God's reality revealed in Christ.[1]

Bonhoeffer had returned from America at the end of the summer, 1939. It was April 1943 when he was arrested. In the three-and-a-half years intervening, besides his work on behalf of the Confessing Church, his increasing involvement with the conspiracy, and falling in love, Bonhoeffer made the time to begin work on what he expected to be his *magnum opus*, a book on ethics.[2]

The chaos of the days, however, prevented the book from being completed. Drafts of various segments of the proposed book were completed, though without notations about the order in which they were to be assembled. It was after the war that Eberhard Bethge organized, edited, and expanded the materials into the book we now call *Ethics*. It is long and challenging, yet like a large uncut diamond, it is invaluable, fascinating, and provocative.

He had once been disappointed by American theologians for having confused theology with ethics. Now he had a chance to write about ethics while laying careful theological foundations. Already involved in the conspiracy, ethical questions weighed heavily on his mind.

Some have argued that Bonhoeffer remained a pacifist and would never have been a part of an assassination attempt.[3] Clearly Bonhoeffer, along with all his family, knew of the existence and the intent of the conspiracy well in advance. And clearly, Bonhoeffer was given an assignment by his brother-in-law, Hans von Dohnanyi, to aid in the conspiracy by being a liaison to leaders of other countries in preparation for the successful overthrow of the Nazis. While Bonhoeffer's role was not directly involved with a specific attempt on Hitler's life, he certainly was a knowing part of the whole conspiracy. Hence, he was not an assassin, but he was part of a conspiracy to kill Hitler. To argue otherwise is to ignore, among other things, Bonhoeffer's very concept of ethics.

The historical context at the end of the 1930s obviously was very different than it had been when he spoke about ethics during his internship in Barcelona in 1928-29. Yet the core of Bonhoeffer's thinking about ethics remained the same: The central concern of ethical thinking and acting is not rules but relationships, not commands but communion with God and with humankind. In the opening lines of *Ethics*, Bonhoeffer writes that our task is not to ask, "How can I be good?" but rather, "What is the will of God" (*DBWE* 6:47). The first leads too often into legalism while the second may well lead to God but is easily abused. Many horrors have been committed in the name of God because people so easily claim God's authorization without first maturing into true godliness of spirit. To live truly and directly in response to the will of God requires maturity and maturity requires time. There are no shortcuts.

It is important that we see why Bonhoeffer rejects questions like, How can I be good? or, How can I do something good? "When the ethical problem presents itself essentially as the question of my own being good and doing good," he says, "the decision has already been made that the self and the world are the ultimate realities" (*DBWE* 5:47). We are not to be the final arbiters of our own decisions, not to be the lords of our own lives.

It has long been a problem in conservative circles that we tend to hold fast to rules about behavior and language, rules by which we try to govern ourselves and judge others, even while preaching a Gospel of grace. This bifurcation remains unresolved in many of our churches. While we claim to be followers of Jesus, our understanding of how to make ethical decisions tends to be very legalistic.

We must remember the biblical portrait of the heart of sin as we see it in the story of Adam and Eve. The temptation was to be like God, *knowing good and evil*. Eve interpreted that as the promise of wisdom. We continue to think that the ability to distinguish good from evil is what empowers us to be good, though history—yours, mine, and human in general—repeatedly proves otherwise. If we recognize the good and choose it for ourselves, we are indeed the lords of our own lives. Certainly choosing the good is better than choosing evil but, as Bonhoeffer sees clearly, it is still sin if it supplants our responsiveness to God.

It is central to Bonhoeffer's thought as well, that we are dealing not with doctrines and principles but with the living and present Lord. Our task is not to do something for God but simply to be faithful followers of Jesus Christ. "For Christian ethics, the mere possibility of knowing about good and evil is already a falling away from the origin. Living in the origin, human beings know nothing but God alone," Bonhoeffer wrote (*DBWE* 6:300).

Even more strongly, Bonhoeffer argues that, "The question of the good becomes the question of participating in God's reality revealed in Christ" *(DBWE* 6:50). He is avoiding the possibility that we might think of ourselves in such distinction from God that "we here" respond to "God over there." It is our communion with God, our harmony with his Spirit, that Bonhoeffer commends. "What matters is *participating in the reality of God and the world in Jesus Christ today*" (*DBWE* 6:55).

If our identity is established by our identification with Jesus Christ and, more deeply, by his identification with us, then *character* matters more than deeds. Bonhoeffer writes provocatively,

> It is worse to be evil than to do evil. It is worse when a liar tells the truth than when a lover of truth lies, worse when a person who hates humanity practices neighborly love than when a loving person once falls victim to hatred. The lie is better than truth in the mouth of a liar, as hatred is better than acts of neighborly love by a misanthrope (*DBWE* 6:77).

No one committed to living by rules and principles can be comfortable with such words. Bonhoeffer is reaching deeper into our psyche than the level of merely deciding whether to do right or do wrong. Who we are in Christ Jesus is more fundamental than what we do. These are dangerous words because they can so easily be twisted into something monstrous such as Nietzsche's *Übermensch*, the one who simply asserts himself above all others. We can understand nothing of Bonhoeffer if we forget that which he never forgot: that our communion with God in Christ Jesus is the central reality of our lives.

Some years ago, when I was in campus ministry in Hawaii, my wife and I attended a newly established congregation led by an ambitious church planter. To inspire us and stir up our ambitions, the pastor invited someone from one of the first megachurches in southern California, now long bankrupt. Over and over again the fellow asked us, "Don't you want to do a great work for God?" He challenged us to "Do something big; do a great work for God." I kept thinking, God spun billions of stars of unimaginably huge size across the universe with a mere word, making any work of mine seem immeasurably small. God needs no great work from us. He just asks faithful responsiveness, no matter the cost.

Faith is the appropriate response to the faithfulness of God. We cannot predict God's call in our lives from day to day and cannot claim to be faithful unless we are listening day by day for the freshness of God's call. The faithful are fully committed not to a plan but to a person, not to a possibility but to a presence. They are not committed to rules of ethics or to theological answers but always and only to the voice of the living Lord. "And your ears shall hear a word behind you, saying, 'This is the way, walk in it,' when you turn to the right or when you turn to the left" (Isaiah 30:21). Notice that Isaiah is not saying we simply sit and wait for the voice. We continue walking in the direction of God's way until he guides us into a new direction. We walk and we wait simultaneously.

Even in 1928 Bonhoeffer was thinking about the story of the Garden of Eden in Genesis 3 (*DBWE* 10:363). The sin was attempting to gain a knowledge of good and evil, right and wrong. We tend to think of differentiating good and evil as the cure when in fact it is the problem. Adam and Eve were given no rules by which to conduct their lives but one: Don't eat the fruit of the tree of knowledge of good and evil. How were they to know what to do? It was clear: All they had to do was walk with God.[4] Ethical systems, on the other hand, presume the absence of God. By assuming we can control our own lives and hearts well enough to meet any standards God may give us, we believe we can be lords of our own lives.

Bonhoeffer understood from the beginning that the image of the Garden, while helpful in protecting us from falling into a "live by the rules" kind of life, could also mislead us into thinking we are perpetually to be children, immature and irresponsible. The innocence of a child is based upon a certain irresponsibility. When we grow up, we become responsible adults. Even the guidance of the Lord does not relieve us of personal responsibility. The Lord guides, but we choose whether to listen or not.

There is a certain paradox here which reveals our confused thinking on this matter. We think of being responsible for ourselves as a mark of maturity, yet it usually entails living either by rules and principles or emotions and whims, either of which is a form of immaturity and irresponsibility. If we lives by rules alone, we are not free; if we live ruled by emotions alone, we often are not responsible. Thus the paradox: to become mature, we strive to be both responsible and free.

There may be times when, as responsible adults, we have to make decisions which in and of themselves may seem immoral. We will not be able to remain innocent in the eyes of the law. In war we may be compelled to kill, for example, though neither war nor killing in war are innocent activities (*DBWE* 10:372). If you are in my home and an evil man comes to the door, seeking to do you harm, rest assured I will lie to protect you.

The theme of responsibility was of great importance to Bonhoeffer. As he contemplated his responses to Hitler over the Nazi years, he had a growing sense of Hitler's evil. When the extent of the Führer's murderous ways became clear, Bonhoeffer realized that to do nothing to jam the wheel of the Nazi state would mean sharing in the responsibility for all those deaths. This was unbearable for him. He accepted the responsibility for the assassination not with a sense of being innocent but of being responsible. The assassination was the most loving and God-honoring choice he could conceive, a responsibility from which he could not retreat.[5] To do nothing to restrain evil is to condone evil by default.

In one section of his notes for *Ethics* there is a passage which he sent separately to Bethge and Dohnanyi under the title "After Ten Years." In it he writes,

> Who stands firm? Only the one whose ultimate standard is not his reason, his principles, conscience, freedom, or virtue; only the one who is prepared to sacrifice all of these when, in faith and in relationship to God alone, he is called to obedience and responsible action. Such a person is the responsible one, whose life is to be nothing but a response to God's question and call. Where are these responsible ones? (*DBWE* 8:40).

The one who truly honors God is not the one with the longest list of virtues but simply the one whose ultimate response is directly to God. That one can be said to be *responsible* to God and God alone. Bonhoeffer seems to be using the term "responsible" in two senses at once. It means both *responsive* to God and *accountable* to God.

So, though he never wavers in his commitment to the absolute sovereignty of God, Bonhoeffer sees that there is a corresponding quality that is necessary in us: personal responsibility. He never drifts into the ultra-pious stance captured in the old cliche, "Let go and let God." God is not responsible for our lives *instead* of us being responsible. We are responsible for our choices. That means both that we are responsible *to God* and at the same time we are responsible *for ourselves and our own decisions*.

Bonhoeffer must have known that there would come a time when a great many Germans would be claiming innocence because they were simply following orders. They would be arguing that they were responsible only for being obedient to their leaders, not for the moral dimensions of the orders they received. And, just as he had anticipated, at the Nuremberg trials following the war, that is precisely the defense offered by many for the horrific evils of the Nazi era. And that is precisely the argument rejected by the courts in Nuremberg. Obedience is not a substitute for personal responsibility. All the world, witnessing that trial, could see the error in the defendants' position.

Long before those trials, Bonhoeffer had seen that we cannot dispense with either dimension—obedience or responsibility—especially in our relationship with God. Responsibility is never nullified by the demand for obedience. And yet, there is something more to what he is saying. This is difficult for evangelicals. Even if we have found some sort of synergy of obedience and personal responsibility, we are still in danger of slipping into an attempt to make ourselves good by trying hard to be obedient and responsible. There is something more, something which perhaps ought to be familiar to evangelicals but is in fact seldom taken seriously or even noticed.

Before we examine this "something more" in Bonhoeffer, let us look with some care at the way it shows up in Scripture, in this line from Galatians, for example:

> I have been crucified with Christ and it is not I who live,
> but it is Christ who lives in me. And the life I now live in

the flesh I live by faith in the Son of God, who loved me and gave himself for me (Galatians 2:19-20).

There are two dimensions to Paul's thought here, though we evangelicals tend to hear only one. The second dimension, the one we like, is that we live by faith. We blow our trumpets loudly and often to remind one another that we are saved by faith and we live by faith. What we don't seem to notice is the first and foundational idea here: We have been crucified with Christ and no longer have our own life. The life that is lived by faith is the very life of Jesus Christ.

We *experience* this as a life of faith and faithful choosing but, if we truly understand the message here, the deeper truth is that we are experiencing *Christ's life*. Christ is living in and through us or, more precisely, in and through our *koinonia*, our fellowship. That's why Bonhoeffer can say that when we pray the Psalms, these are not our prayers but Christ's.[6] It is why he can say with Paul that the church is the body of Christ. Consider when Paul asks in Romans:

> Should we continue in sin in order that grace may abound? By no means! How can we who died to sin go on living in it? Do you not know that all of us who have been baptized into Christ Jesus were baptized into his death? Therefore we have been buried with him by baptism into death, so that, just as Christ was raised from the dead by the glory of the Father, so we too might walk in newness of life. For if we have been united with him in a death like his, we will certainly be united with him in a resurrection like his. We know that our old self was crucified with him so that the body of sin might be destroyed, and we might no longer be enslaved to sin. For whoever has died is freed from sin. But if we have died with Christ, we believe that we will also live with him. We know that Christ, being raised from the dead, will never die again; death no longer has dominion over him. The death he died, he died to sin, once for all; but the life he lives, he lives to God. So you also must consider yourselves dead to sin and alive to God in Christ Jesus (Romans 6:1-11).

Notice that Paul does not say we are to refrain from sin because we are too virtuous or too obedient to allow ourselves to sin. No, we refrain from sin because sin is an expression of our old, crucified, dead-and-gone self. It has been buried with us as we have been dead and buried with Jesus Christ. And, having been crucified with Christ, we shall certainly be raised from the dead with him.

I seldom hear much emphasis upon this idea in my evangelical circles. I suppose in part it is because we have so commonly held to a view of the Cross from the doctrine of Substitutionary Atonement which, while not in error, is at least inadequate. It is the idea that Jesus died on the Cross *in our place.* The Bible, however, is clear: we are on the Cross with Jesus. To be a follower of Jesus is not to escape the Cross but to take it up. Jesus said, "If any want to become my followers, let them deny themselves and take up their cross and follow me. For those who want to save their life will lose it, and those who lose their life for my sake, and for the sake of the gospel, will save it" (Mark 8:34-35).

At the crucifixion of Jesus Christ, all the world—including you and me—was united in venting our hatred of God onto the seemingly helpless, defenseless Christ. We meant it to be destructive, completing the rejection of God begun in the Garden, but God in grace transformed the moment into quite the opposite. "The world exhausts its rage on the body of Jesus Christ. But the martyred one forgives the world its sins. Thus reconciliation takes place" (*DBWE* 6:83). Jesus Christ accepted without resistance our rage, our hatred, our sin—and forgave us. That is the transforming reconciliation. The appropriate response is to accept our place on the cross with Jesus Christ, as if stepping out from the crowd and its jeering to feel the nails piercing our own bodies. We can identify with Jesus Christ because he has first identified with us.

We cannot evade the cross and simply accept the life of the resurrected Christ. The path to life in Christ leads first to the cross and our death with Christ. We cannot say our own sin has been too minor to have contributed to his death. Sin is not quantified in the heart of God. "There is no calculating here. I must acknowledge that my own sin is to blame for all these things" (*DBWE* 6:136), whether the Cross of Christ or the poisoning of the life of the church or the mission of the church into the world. We each and all must bear responsibility for our sin and humbly submit it and our whole hearts to the Cross for continual reconciliation.

When we study Romans 6, we are made uncomfortable because we know that, in fact, we do still sin. We still fall short of the glory of

God. But Paul is talking about something else here. Not our experience but our reality: We are dead and buried with Christ, then raised to life so that—in the words of Galatians—"it is no longer I who live but Christ who lives in me." Followers of Jesus Christ follow him on *his* path (rather than asking him to bless us on *our* path). And that path leads to the cross, to crucifixion, to death.

Bonhoeffer, taking such biblical ideas deeply into his own heart, insists there is nothing we can do to make ourselves good. Neither hard work nor self-discipline nor even great faith will *make* us good. Goodness or, to be more biblical in our terms, righteousness is never ours but always and only Christ's, always and only a gracious gift to us and never our own possession. We are righteous *in Christ* and we live *in Christ*, never on our own or by our own strength or virtue.

We've seen such thinking in Bonhoeffer earlier. He insisted, for example, in *Life Together*, that in Christian fellowship we never meet one another directly but only *in Christ*. Our communion with Christ may be a mystery but it is simple: we are who we are only in Jesus Christ and we are ourselves only in Christ together. This is fundamental to Bonhoeffer's thought at least from the time of his doctoral dissertation, *The Communion of Saints*. As Clifford Green noted, "In *Sanctorum Communio* . . . the central theological category is the concept of person—a concept that is both individual and corporate. Person in this first work is defined in ethical terms,"[7] and thus becomes central also to *Ethics*.

Jesus was baptized by John in a "baptism of repentance for the forgiveness of sins" (Mark 1:4), though he had no sin of his own. He identified with us and with our sin. On the cross Jesus accepted for himself the death that was due us. He called us to identify with him on the cross *in our sinful state*. If we are followers of Jesus, are we not also to identify not with the great and powerful but with those trapped in weakness and sin?

This is often not the evangelical church I know. We want to call people out from their sin but we call them from across a gulf that separates us. We want to share with them the Good News of God's grace and forgiveness but only if they can bridge the gulf by straightening out their lives. Our love is thus conditional, depending upon their change to be like us. We did not learn such an attitude from our Lord.

Bonhoeffer writes in very strong, even shocking words:

> In an incomprehensible reversal of all righteous and pious thought, God declares himself as guilty toward the world and thereby extinguishes the guilt of the world. God treads the way of humble reconciliation and thereby sets the world free. God wills to be guilty of our guilt; God takes on the punishment and suffering that guilt has brought on us. God takes responsibility for godlessness, love for hate, the holy one for the sinner. Now there is no more godlessness, hate, or sin that God has not taken upon himself, suffered, and atoned. Now there is no longer any reality, any world, that is not reconciled with God and at peace. God has done this in the beloved son, Jesus Christ. Ecce homo! *(DBWE 5:83)*.

These are hard words to read, though the Cross makes no sense if they are not true. Ours is the guilt and ours should be the resulting punishment, but God in Christ Jesus receives and accepts into himself all the sin, the evil, the hatred of the human heart—and the death which they bring.

We are called not just to believe the reality Bonhoeffer is expressing but to honor it, and not only to honor it but to live it. Followers of Christ must go where he goes and must go to whom he goes. We are to love the way Christ loves and be gracious as he is gracious, because ours *is* the life of Christ.

Try as we might, we Christians have not yet found a viable way to distinguish ourselves from the Pharisees[8] with whom Jesus tangled so fiercely and frequently. They seemed always to be in each other's way because in one important dimension they were in agreement: Both Jesus and the Pharisees cared deeply about personal righteousness. Their great differences were in how they answered the question, How does one become righteous? For the Pharisees, righteousness was attained by close adherence to Torah and the traditions by which Torah was explicated. For Jesus, righteousness was a gift given in gracious forgiveness. For the Pharisees, righteousness was a goal, while for Jesus it was the starting point.

Far too commonly, we Christians have tended to promote a rules-centered lifestyle, even when we have called it something else, such as a "values-generated" agenda.

A rulebook of ethics accomplishes little beyond giving us some basis for judging and condemning one another. Legalists tend to commend themselves and condemn others. The spirit of judgment thrives in an environment of legalism.

Just as importantly, the mindset built around rules or "principles," as we like to say these days, tends to stifle growth, learning, developing. The Pharisees saw themselves and their traditions as "building a fence around the law." They wanted to *define* Torah, to clarify its extent and, by implication, its limits. Too easily, such thinking fences us in and corrals our creativity. The children of the Creator, created in the very image of the Creator, ought by nature to be the most creative people on earth. Or so one would think.

Another fruit of the pharisaical mind is that it restricts us to thinking in terms only of personal righteousness and excludes from our purview the crucial concern for justice. It is perhaps to our disadvantage that we so easily dissociate justice and righteousness. The one seems social while the other seems individual. Even worse, having thought of justice and righteousness as distinct from one another, evangelicals have tended to dismiss justice as being someone else's concern while we "righteous" folk give our attention to making one another more righteous. Our main tool in that job, of course, is the spirit of judgment and condemnation by which we punish wrongdoing.

What we need to bear in mind is that the New Testament set of words built around the root *dik* includes righteous, righteousness, just, justice, justification, justify, and so on. The New Testament does not support any sort of distinction between justice and righteousness.

Furthermore, a large portion of the Hebrew Bible is devoted to the work of the prophets. The words "Moses" and "law" are rare in the messages of the prophets. They called Israel to righteousness with scant reference to Torah. Amos, for example, in the famous list of accusations against the people of the region (chapters 1-2), speaks five times of "righteous" or "righteousness" but has no occurrence of "Torah." The prophets were calling for a higher righteousness than the Hebrews were finding in Torah at the time. Here is part of Amos' call against Israel:

> Thus says the LORD: For three transgressions of Israel, and for four, I will not revoke the punishment; because they sell the righteous for silver, and the needy for a pair of sandals-- they who trample the head of the poor into the dust of the earth, and push the afflicted out of the way. (Amos 2:6-7).

We should be frightened by such words because they describe contemporary America. If we do not protest and actively resist the rapidly growing disparity between the wealth of the few and the deteriorating situation of the majority, we are not in harmony with God's prophets.

Following rules seems to us to be easier than to follow a living Lord. It is not just that we fear the cost of walking Jesus' path. It is more common to have the feeling that Jesus is walking too far ahead of us for us to see our way clearly. Or perhaps we could say that the guiding Spirit of the Lord is just too subtle for us, speaking in such a still, small voice that we cannot quite hear.

Bible, prayer, fellowship: these are the staples of American and British evangelicalism and yet we are the ones too easily drawn into a pharisaical commitment to rules and regulations. Was there some fourth factor Bonhoeffer had in mind to protect us from legalism? Or, was there something about those three which differed from what we might expect?

As I ask such questions, only one thing comes to mind: confession. When Bonhoeffer describes the Christian community, he had in mind a community grounded in personal confession one to another, as we saw in our discussion of *Life Together*. Evangelicals have produced hundreds of self-help books in the last half-century but seldom is the word "confession" to be found in them. Is that what we need? Is that what makes the difference? Are we simply not honest enough with each other, not trusting enough of each other? Does our faith in Christ remain incomplete until it becomes also a trust in each other? Have we not yet fully entrusted ourselves to Jesus Christ if we have not entrusted ourselves to our brothers and sisters in the faith?

As little Billy, whom we met in Chapter 4, said, "When someone loves you, the way they say your name is different. You just know that your name is safe in their mouth." That is exactly what Bonhoeffer sees as essential to the church. It can only be true when we are in relationships where we know and are known, where we are safe not because our sins are hidden but because they are known and forgiven. The words "I love you" have little meaning unless they convey a broader message: "I see you; I know you; I love you."

When we speak of "fellowship" we too often mean the coffee hour between two morning services. Or our occasional potluck suppers. Eugene Peterson has a better view, one that incorporates Bonhoeffer's expectation that we are to be a fellowship bound together by confession. Peterson speaks of the three fundamentals of ministry—or three angles, as he calls them—as Prayer, Scripture, and Spiritual Direction. By "spiritual direction" he does not mean one person telling another which spiritual exercises to follow. "Spiritual direction," he writes, "takes place when two people agree to give their full attention to what God is doing in one (or both) of their lives and seek to respond in faith."[9] Spiritual direction, in other words, is just a matter of two people listening for the voice of the Spirit in one another. We listen; we name; we thank God.

Dietrich Bonhoeffer spoke of spiritual formation as meaning "in the first place Jesus Christ taking form in Christ's church. Here it is the very form of Jesus Christ that takes form" (*DBWE* 5:96). What we are hearing when we listen for the voice of the Spirit in another person is the Spirit of God speaking the word of creation, forming the very person of Jesus Christ in the fellowship and in the hearts of God's people.

"Ethics as formation is possible only on the basis of the form of Jesus Christ present in Christ's church," Bonhoeffer wrote. "The church is the place where Jesus Christ's taking form is proclaimed and where it happens" (*DBWE* 5:102). Bonhoeffer is taking with full seriousness Paul's idea that the church is the body of Christ.

Dietrich Bonhoeffer thus has come full circle. He began his serious theological work with an exploration of the church as *Communio Sanctorum*, the communion of saints, and now speaks of ethics as the process of the character of Jesus Christ being formed in the fellowship of the believers in the church.

What work is left to do? Bonhoeffer in *Ethics* has already begun the theological work which will occupy his mind for several fruitful months while he is imprisoned: The relation of the church to the world. "What matters," he wrote, "is participating in the reality of God and the world in Jesus Christ today. And doing so in such a way that I never experience the reality of God without the reality of the world, nor the reality of the world without the reality of God" (*DBWE* 6:55).

He has warned us that to consider the world from the perspective of the living Christ is to see the world from the Cross of Christ. "The body of Jesus Christ, especially as it is presented to us on the cross, makes visible to faith both the world in its sin and in its being loved by God, and the church-community as the company of those who recognize their sin and gratefully submit to the love of God" (*DBWE* 6:68). The Cross tells us both what we and the world deserve and what we and the world are to God: beloved, valued, cherished.

What more will he be saying in his famous *Letters and Papers from Prison*? It is there that he plunges more fully than ever into our participation not just in one another's hearts, not just into our communion with Jesus Christ, but into our participation with the world.

Endnotes

1   *DBWE* 6:50.

2   It is important to note that in Bonhoeffer's mind, the capstone of his theological work was not to be a systematic theology. That would have been a book of ideas about God. Instead, it was to be a book on ethics, a book on our responses to God. The theological foundation was important, of course.

3   Mark Thiessen Nation, Anthony G. Siegrist, and Daniel P Umbel, *Bonhoeffer the Assassin?: Challenging the Myth, Recovering His Call to Peacemaking* (Grand Rapids: Baker Academic, 2013), argue that Bonhoeffer never diminished in his commitment to pacifism and did not participate in the plot to assassinate Hitler, though he knew of it.

4   Bonhoeffer always resisted the temptation to dwell extensively on our experience in the Garden before eating the forbidden fruit. In his lectures on Genesis 1—3, published as *Creation and Fall*, he had insisted, "The attempt—with the origin and nature of humankind in mind—to take a gigantic leap back into the world of the lost beginning, to seek to know for ourselves what humankind was like in its original state and to identify our own ideal of humanity with what God actually created is hopeless. It fails to recognize that it is only from Christ that we can know about the original nature of humankind" (*DBWE* 3:62).

5   Karen Guth warns us away from merely using Bonhoeffer's choice to join the conspiracy as justification for taking the law into our own hands whenever we disagree with someone: "What if, rather than asking 'What would Bonhoeffer do?' or claiming Bonhoeffer for our cause, we instead asked ourselves the central questions of his life: 'Who is Christ actually for *us* today?' and how may Christ 'take form among *us* today and here?'" She says, "Bonhoeffer is indeed a moral role model—but less in the sense of providing concrete instruction than in reminding Christians of the constantly shifting nature of discipleship and the need for humility." Karen V. Guth, "Claims on Bonhoeffer: The Misuse of a Theologian," *Christian Century*, May 27, 2015: 26ff.

6   *Prayerbook of the Bible: An Introduction to the Psalms, DBWE* 5: 157.

7   Clifford Green, Editor's Introduction to *Ethics, DBWE*:6:3.

8   When we speak of the Pharisees, we need always to remember that, however much they clashed with Jesus, they would soon become those who remained most firm in holding the faith after the fall of Jerusalem and the loss of the Temple. They were the foundation on which the famous "Rabbinic Judaism" was built.

9   Eugene Peterson, *Working the Angles* (Grand Rapids: Wm. B. Eerdmans Publishing Co., 1987), 103f.

CHAPTER SEVEN

Letters and Papers from Prison

Before God and with God, we live without God.[1]

On April 5, 1943, Maria von Wedemeyer, having been engaged to Bonhoeffer for less than three months but not having seen him during that time, made an odd entry in her diary: "Has something bad happened? I'm afraid it must be something very bad."[2] Clearly, her heart was fully intertwined with that of her beloved Dietrich.

On that day, 150 miles to the east at the Bonhoeffer home in Berlin, Dietrich was arrested and placed in Tegel Prison on charges of "subversion of the armed forces." Before long it became clear that the Gestapo had found some financial irregularities in the movement of a handful of Jews to Switzerland. Bonhoeffer, working with Dohnanyi, had arranged for visas and papers for them. His role in the conspiracy was not known and was not the cause for his arrest.[3]

It seems to have taken a full year for the shock to wear off so that Bonhoeffer could effectively return to his intellectual and spiritual work. When the time came and his mind and heart awakened again, he entered a brief period of deep and creative work.

The Early Letters

Those who have dwelt attentively on the life and writings of Bonhoeffer up to this point will find that, arriving at these letters, we have hit emotional and theological paydirt. At last, it seems, Bonhoeffer is free to state directly those deepest ideas toward which his mind and heart have been leaning throughout his adult life. The seeds that were sown as far back as his lectures in Barcelona, for example, now bear full fruit in his cell at Tegel prison. Many of these prison letters are especially rich, rewarding, and of course challenging.

The Theological Letters

The most important theological letters were written from April through July of 1944, with the last penned on July 21, the day after the failed attempt on Hitler's life. That surely is no coincidence. Hitler may have survived the attack but perhaps for Bonhoeffer, hope did not. It may be that now he hoped only for that which awaited him beyond the grave.[4] Though there are a few letters written after that point, they do not seem to come from a growing edge, from a movement forward. So it is the letters from that one key four-month period that draw our deepest attention.

It is often noted that christology was always of central importance in Bonhoeffer's thought. I think that is not quite right. It was not christology (the study of the doctrines of Christ) but Christ himself who remained the steady hub of Bonhoeffer's rapidly turning life and thought. Writing to Eberhard Bethge (as he does in all the letters we'll examine) on April 22, 1944, Bonhoeffer wrote:

> There are people who change, and many who can hardly change at all. I don't think I have ever changed much, except perhaps at the time of my first impressions abroad, and under the first conscious influence of Papa's personality. It was then that a turning from the phraseological to the real ensued (*DBWE* 8:358).

Bonhoeffer and his siblings remained impressed all their lives by their father's insistence on careful articulation of ideas with no jargon and no circuitous reasoning. Bonhoeffer now seems to connect his father's dictum with his own realization that there is a distinction to be made between reality and our attempts to express or describe it. Theology at that point ceased to be merely a matter of words and ideas and became for Bonhoeffer an endeavor to reach behind the words to the very realities of God.

It was a fad a few years ago to ask, "What would Jesus do?" Bonhoeffer would have had little patience with such a question because it implies an absent Jesus. Instead, he was asking, "What *is* Jesus doing and how can I be following?" We walk *with* the living and present Jesus Christ, not instead of him.

When Bonhoeffer first got to be with Karl Barth, meeting him in person and attending some of his lectures and classes, he was deeply impressed, not merely by Barth's ideas but by his persona. He wrote to his friend Erwin Sutz that Barth "stands beyond his books." He went on to say:

> I am impressed by his discussion even more than by his writing and lectures. He is really fully present. I have never seen anything like it nor thought it possible. At the end, he said he thought I was making grace into a principle and was bludgeoning everything else to death with it (*DBWE* 11:37).

That is exactly what Bonhoeffer sought in his relationship to God, to know that the Lord is *fully present.* Yes, we learn a great deal from and about Barth from his writings, just as we learn a great deal from and about God from Scripture, but there is no substitute for the sense of presence which so powerfully moves us beyond the verbal or ideological to the real person.

Notice, though, that Bonhoeffer had not yet learned the lesson very fully because, as Barth himself pointed out, grace was for Bonhoeffer first and foremost a principle. It would not take young Bonhoeffer long to outgrow this mistake. Grace soon ceased to be a doctrine and became instead the spiritual air Bonhoeffer breathed.

Years later, writing from his prison cell, Bonhoeffer reveals another of his characteristics, the lifelong habit of asking questions. Rather than clinging like a desperate man to the few answers of which he was certain, Bonhoeffer kept reaching ahead for new understanding. Answers may give us an illusion of security while questions bring risk. Answers close doors while questions are the keys to opening them. "A wise interrogating is half a knowledge," said Francis Bacon long ago.[5] Questions pull us from half an answer to a whole answer which, if it is a good answer, raises more questions.

A fundamentalist is one whose heart has become hardened, encrusted by right answers in theology and right rules in ethics, unable to ask questions or raise doubts. Not intimidated by the bars that surrounded him in prison, Bonhoeffer dared to ask the biggest questions he could imagine.

On April 30, Bonhoeffer wrote, "What keeps gnawing at me is the question, what is Christianity, or who is Christ actually for us today? (*DBWE* 8:362). The question echoes that which the disciples of Jesus asked long ago: "Who then is this, that even wind and sea obey him?" (Mark 4:41). Always a careful student of the Bible, Bonhoeffer was deeply conscious of the lessons about Jesus contained in the Gospels but he never believed those Gospels established the parameters of our knowledge of Christ. After all, the Gospels themselves point beyond the life of Jesus, beyond the cross and the tomb, to the time of resurrection when the Spirit will continue the presence and the teaching which is witnessed in the Gospels.

Notice that Bonhoeffer considers the two questions to be equivalent in some sense: What is Christianity? Who is Christ actually for us today? For Bonhoeffer, there is no meaningful Christianity that is not centered precisely in Jesus Christ, so to ask about one is to ask about the other. The reason such questions seem important to Bonhoeffer at this time is his observation about the world which surrounds him, not just in prison but in the whole of Germany:

> The age when we could tell people [who Jesus is] with words—whether with theological or with pious words—is past, as is the age of inwardness and of conscience, and that means the age of religion altogether. We are approaching a completely religionless age; people as they are now simply cannot be religious anymore (*DBWE* 8:362).

These words are only now coming into focus for us in America.[6] We have continued to be a religious people and the number of people identifying themselves as Christian, Jew, Muslim, or just "spiritual" is greater than it was at the end of World War II. The numbers, though, seem to be a bit less than they were ten years ago. Something is slipping. More seriously, the number of people who openly claim no allegiance to a church and even no belief in God is growing rapidly. Atheists, it seems, sell more books than Christians these days. Now we are realizing that Bonhoeffer was seeing well into the future, our future!

One of the reasons why Christians in America are being excluded from the public forum is that they keep talking about God and the Bible as if these were values shared by all people. We seem to think that if we say God cares about this or that, everyone should pay attention. In fact, the majority of people don't care at all about what we say God wants for us because they neither believe we speak for God—we've lost our credibility—nor even believe in the biblical portrait of God at all. "Caught as we are, somewhere between modernity and marginality,"[7] we are both too entangled in modernity (and now post-modernity) to have anything unique to say and too marginalized to be heard anyway. Returning to our biblical foundations is the only realistic option. We hear the Word, speak the Word, and entrust the Word to the Spirit who alone enlivens it in the hearts of those who listen.

It is essential that we learn how to communicate with the world around us. Walter Brueggemann argues that "people of faith in public life must be *bilingual*. They must have *a public language*" and "a more *communal language* for use behind the gate, in the community."[8] Emily Dickenson was right when she observed that the whole truth, told too bluntly, can be damaging and more difficult to hear. We remember what Paul wrote to the Ephesians that we grow up by speaking the truth in love. Some people forget the love and while they may be speaking the truth, they use it as a club to beat others into submission. Thus as Dickenson says, "Tell all the Truth but tell it slant...The Truth must dazzle gradually or every man be blind."[9]

The matter of the creation of the universe is a case in point. Fundamentalists are sure that the Genesis stories in chapters 1—3 give us a more accurate picture of creation than does science. They expend enormous amounts of time and energy defending Genesis against science, thereby disqualifying themselves from participation in the public forum because they are arguing on grounds the general public simply do not accept.

Recently my wife and I watched a PBS rerun on the European Space Agency's project to land a sophisticated box of equipment on a comet. The flight took ten years and, to build sufficient speed, had to circle the earth twice and Mars once. That equipment is now on the comet, billions of miles from earth. I am staggered as I try to imagine how in the world we could achieve such of feat.

Science is truly amazing but it is not the enemy of God. I suspect the Creator, who gave us the mandate to rule the world in his image, in his own way, must be delighted at how well we are doing at exploring his creation.

Science is just figuring out how God created the universe, whether or not that's what the scientists think as they work. If we had kept Genesis 1—3 as the fence around whatever science could do, what could science have done? And when Christians argue that science must not contradict some particular interpretation of Genesis, no wonder they are told to shut up and get out of the way.

Not long ago I was choosing a new cell phone. I told the clerk that all I wanted was a phone to use for talking with people. He showed me a model that had a camera, a light, internet access, and I think maybe a bottle opener and several other features that were of no interest to me. I reminded him that all I wanted to do was listen and talk. He showed me another model and listed all its features. I reminded him that none of those features were of value to me. So he picked up another and told me all I could do with it. By then, I was pretty frustrated that he was unable to hear me. We Christians are often like that ourselves, talking about religious matters to people who do not care about religious matters. And we frustrate them with our refusal to listen.

Bonhoeffer was not interested in finding ways to make people religious again. He never had been. Even when he was in Spain in 1928, he had written to his parents, "I think that dumb saying about the stultification of the masses through religion really does find some justification here"[10] (*DBWE* 10:99). And in a 1932 sermon he spoke very strongly about this:

> Our disobedience is not that we are so little religious but that we actually would like very much to be religious, [to] find it very edifying, when someone somewhere says and writes: "In the name of God, Amen," [and we] are very much reassured when some government or other proclaims the Christian worldview. It is our disobedience, it is our fleeing, it is our calamitous downfall—that we, the more pious we are, are all the less willing to let ourselves be told that God is dangerous; that God does not allow himself to be mocked; that we human beings must die if we really want to have anything to do with the living God; that we must lose our life if we really want to gain it; that we must be baptized not only with water but also with fire and [the] Spirit; that this "In the name of God, Amen," if it really is to have any meaning and not be just empty talk, is a majestic region that one can enter only as a completely captive slave—or not at all (*DBWE* 11:455).

Religion is safe; God is dangerous. Religion makes us feel secure; God terrifies us. The friendship of the Lord is offered *only* to those who fear him (Psalm 25:14).

Bonhoeffer had said that "ethics is a matter of blood and a matter of history. . . . It is a child of the earth. . ." (*DBWE* 10:360). That is to say, ethics is shaped by culture and context. He could use identical words to describe religion. Religion is a cultural chameleon, changing to match its context in various times and places. The old British historian Herbert Butterfield observed, however, that:

> while men weep to see the end of the things they love, something in Christianity survives the fall of Roman Empires and national monarchies, lives on when Platonism and Aristotelianism go out of fashion, and persists when a whole civilization changes its character. The Christian is particularly called to carry his thinking outside that framework which a nation or a political party or a social system or an accepted regime or a mundane ideology provides.[11]

We must remind ourselves here that it was in the fall of 1928, while in Barcelona, that Bonhoeffer had said, "Christianity contains a seed of animosity to the church since we wish to base a demand on God on our devotion to Christ and church" (*DBWE* 10:52). Religion too easily slips into a way of trying to manipulate God, of doing this or that little thing just right so that God will be obligated to bless us or at least not demand too much of us. So, whatever else one may wish to say about Bonhoeffer's call to move beyond religion in 1944, we must see that his "religionless Christianity" is not a new thought but has been brewing in his mind for at least sixteen years.

The incarnation of the Word of God—the birth of Jesus the Christ—is of fundamental significance for us. He was born in a stable, not in the Temple. He was laid in a feeding trough, not in a sanctuary. We, then, the followers of Christ, must not retreat into a religious gated community of Jello salads and tater tot hotdish, as we in Minnesota might do. We are to follow Christ not just into the sweetly scented rose garden but into the manure-smelling stables of the world.

Bonhoeffer was ready to move ahead, accepting today's religionless reality without trying to turn back the calendar to religious times. So he asks the next question: "How can Christ become Lord of the religionless as well?" (*DBWE* 8:363). That is precisely the question we evangelicals must ask if we are to regain the ability to have a meaningful conversation with the world and to take our place in the public forum.

We never read of Jesus trying to make people more religious. We see him on several occasions relating to Gentiles and even then he does not try to convert them to Judaism before blessing them. When he does call them to change it is to stop sinning, as in John 8, or to give away their wealth, as in Mark 10, or to stop rejecting the Scripture they claimed to revere, as in Mark 7.

I've never thought of Bonhoeffer's call to a religionless Christianity as being especially shocking. I recall, for instance, that when I became a Christian more than half a century ago, one of the sayings I heard often in my evangelical circles was that Christianity is not a religion but a relationship, a relationship with Jesus Christ. I liked the saying then and I like it now. So when I read Bonhoeffer saying that religion was losing its grip on the West, I found myself thinking, "Good riddance to religion."

I also recall those months before I became a believer, months in which I read the New Testament over and over again, especially the Gospels. One of the many things that impressed me about Jesus was that he got along so well with so many different people, all except the religious folk. My reading of the Gospels left me with a strong sense that religion can be a serious threat to one's relation with God. It seemed to me then, as it does now, that religion is our way of trying to appease or even manipulate God.

Bonhoeffer has a different and very challenging critique of religion:

> Religious people speak of God at a point where human knowledge is at an end (or sometimes when they're too lazy to think further), or when human strength fails. Actually, it's a deus ex machina[12] that they're always bringing on the scene, either to appear to solve insoluble problems or to provide strength when human powers fail, thus always exploiting human weakness or human limitations. Inevitably that lasts only until human beings become powerful enough to push the boundaries a bit further and God is no longer needed as deus ex machina (*DBWE* 8:366).

Most of our evangelism in America for the last two centuries has been need-centered. We identify people's perceived needs and speak a word about God as mostly the one who meets our needs. The problem with such evangelism is obvious: people who become Christians in order to meet their own needs tend to remain self-centered Christians. The very phrase is nonsense: There can be no such thing as a self-centered follower of Jesus Christ. Often, if a need is met, Jesus is then retired, no longer "needed."

A further problem with the notion that God's primary function is to enter our lives as rescuer is that it reverses the biblical truth that the initiative is always God's. He does not wait for us to get ourselves into a jam and cry out for deliverance. The word Isaiah hears from the Lord is that, "Before they call I will answer, while they are yet speaking I will hear" (Isaiah 65:24).

Ole Hallesby wrote one of the great classics on the spiritual life, called simply *Prayer*. His beginning point is Revelation 3:20: "Listen! I am standing at the door, knocking; if you hear my voice and open the door, I will come in to you and eat with you, and you with me." The great lesson here, says Hallesby, is that "it is not our prayer which moves the Lord Jesus. It is Jesus who moves us to pray."[13]

Bonhoeffer dismisses all thinking which puts God at the edge of our lives, leaving God a role only as one who makes occasional intrusions to fix this or that. He sees a different way.

> I'd like to speak of God not at the boundaries but in the center, not in weakness but in strength, thus not in death and guilt but in human life and human goodness. When I reach my limits, it seems to me better not to say anything and to leave what can't be solved unsolved (*DBWE* 8:366).

God is not that which lies beyond us but that One who is at the center, not of the religious or particularly weak people, but of all life, religious or irreligious, weak or strong. "The church stands not at the point where human powers fail, at the boundaries, but in the center of the village" (*DBWE* 8:367). There is our challenge. How do we stand with God in the center? "What does a church, a congregation, a sermon, a liturgy, a Christian life, mean in a religionless world?" (*DBWE* 8.364).

On May 5 Bonhoeffer again wrote to Bethge, taking up the question, "What then does it mean to 'interpret religiously?'"

> It means, in my opinion, to speak metaphysically, on the one hand, and, on the other hand, individualistically. Neither way is appropriate, either for the biblical message or

> for people today. Hasn't the individualistic question of saving our personal souls almost faded away for most of us? Isn't it our impression that there are really more important things than this question (perhaps not more important than this matter, but certainly more important than the question!)? I know it sounds outrageous to say that, but after all, isn't it fundamentally biblical? Does the question of saving one's soul even come up in the Old Testament? Isn't God's righteousness and kingdom on earth the center of everything? And isn't Rom. 3:24ff the culmination of the view that God alone is righteous, rather than an individualistic doctrine of salvation? (*DBWE* 8:372).

Neither philosophy nor merely personal piety capture the biblical message. And neither alternative can speak to the world which no longer cares about the academic field of theology or about a private sense of devotion to Jesus Christ. Even the question of salvation is of diminishing interest today. As a new Christian I was taught that the Gospel is the story of how I can be saved. I believed that definition for awhile but only until I concluded it didn't actually fit well with the Bible. I was puzzled that I could find so little of the "Gospel" in the Gospels. It took me some time to conclude that I had simply been taught a Gospel which, while not unbiblical, was not from the center of Scripture. Yes, we are saved from death to life in Christ Jesus and we are forgiven our sins in Christ Jesus and justified in Christ Jesus, but none of that truth about the benefits we receive can supplant Christ himself as the center of God's self-revelation.

The Gospel is foremost about Jesus Christ, not about me. The *fruit* of the Gospel includes my salvation, yes, but the *substance* of the Gospel is about the very question Bonhoeffer asks: Who is Jesus Christ? God's righteousness and kingdom on earth is the center of everything.

In late May Bonhoeffer wrote an extended essay on the occasion of the baptism of Eberhard and Renate Bethge's baby, whom they named Dietrich. In it he bemoans the naivete with which the resistors first challenged the Nazis:

> We believed we could make our way in life with reason and justice, and when both failed us, we no longer saw any way forward. We have also overestimated, time and

again, the importance of reasonableness and justice in influencing the course of history. You who are growing up in the midst of a world war, which 90 percent of humankind doesn't want but for which they are giving their lives and goods, will learn from childhood on that this world is ruled by forces against which reason can do nothing (*DBWE* 8:388).

In the beginning, while realizing that Hitler and his followers were highly dangerous, Bonhoeffer's circle was sure that if they simply articulated the truth carefully and clearly, the reasonableness of their position would disarm Hitler by showing the insanity of his ideas. In his loss of innocence, Bonhoeffer now knows that "this world is ruled by forces against which reason can do nothing" (*DBWE* 8:388).

Even at this late date Bonhoeffer retains a clear hope for the future of the church. He is sure that by the time young Dietrich grows up, "the form of the church will have changed considerably" (*DBWE* 8:389). His hope has not yet been fulfilled. His conviction about what the Christians were to be doing in the meantime was very simple and it remains important for us to hear:

> So the words we used before must lose their power, be silenced, and we can be Christians today in only two ways, through prayer and in doing justice among the human beings. All Christian thinking, talking, and organizing must be born anew, out of that prayer and action (*DBWE* 8:389).

Prayer and righteous action.[14] Eugene Peterson rightly says, in harmony with Bonhoeffer, that, "Prayer is the pivotal action in the Christian community."[15] We are to be praying for the world and for the new form of the church, which even today we cannot quite imagine. And we are to speak for justice in our world. In truth, advocating and working for justice, along with prayer, was all Bonhoeffer could envision for the church in this post war period in which we still find ourselves.

On May 29, Bonhoeffer returned to the idea that we must grow beyond our common misunderstanding that God is simply one of the tools in our chest, the one we call upon when none of our other resources seem to work. We should not think of God as merely that which explains what is beyond our understanding and beyond our own ability. When we do so, he said:

> [W]hen the boundaries of knowledge are pushed ever further, God too is pushed further away and thus is ever on the retreat. We should find God in what we know, not in what we don't know; God wants to be grasped by us not in unsolved questions but in those that have been solved. This is true of the relation between God and scientific knowledge, but it is also true of the universal human questions about death, suffering, and guilt. Today, even for these questions, there are human answers that can completely disregard God. Human beings cope with these questions practically without God and have done so throughout the ages, and it is simply not true that only Christianity would have a solution to them (*DBWE* 8:406).

Evangelicals often engage in strenuous debates about the stories of creation in Genesis. Are we to believe Genesis literally even when it cannot be reconciled with contemporary science? To Bonhoeffer, that is not a very important question. We are to let science answer its own questions without using the Bible to place artificial limits of what is or is not legitimate.

It is critical, Bonhoeffer suggests, that we stop thinking of the Creator as no more than the answer to the unanswerable, the solution to the unsolvable. Whatever God may do outside and beyond human comprehension remains incomprehensible, of course, but we cannot allow ourselves to be fixated on "God the magician," the one who specializes only in doing the impossible. As human ingenuity expands the circle of the possible, there seems to be less and less for God to do. What is essential, then, is that we see God in the midst, not at the edges, of human understanding and power.[16]

One source of great difficulty for us as evangelicals is that we think of our relationship to the world primarily in terms of finding ways to get the world to come into the church. As Ray Anderson points out, "Denominations are religious institutions at the edge of the world; the church is an incarnational presence in the midst of the world."[17] The church is simply not the church when it timidly stands on the sidelines and shyly beckons people to come over to it.

June 6, the day the Allied invasion of Normandy began, finds Bonhoeffer immediately aware of the news. He writes to Bethge,

Just to experience this day with you, and in some way with all of you together, I'm hurrying to write you this note. It wasn't a surprise to me, but still, facts are entirely different from expectations. The Daily Text and the interpretative verse call us all to the center of the Gospel—"redemption" is the word around which everything turns. In faith, during the coming weeks, and with great assurance to meet our common future, let us confidently commit your path and all our paths to God. *Caris kai eirhnh!* [Grace and peace] (*DBWE* 8:422).

He knew, of course, that this was the beginning of the end for Germany. Probably no one could have expected that it would take another eleven months for Berlin to fall but the outcome was no longer in doubt. While Bonhoeffer did in fact grieve for his beloved Germany, he knew the coming loss was Germany's only hope.

Notice that even in this momentous time, Bonhoeffer's mind is on the Moravian devotional with its daily readings. More substantial and more important than the unfolding of history was the Gospel and its central message of redemption.[18] The basic text for the day was Psalm 38:4, "For my iniquities have gone over my head; they weigh like a burden too heavy for me." The supplementary text was Ephesians 1:7, "In him we have redemption through his blood, the forgiveness of our trespasses, according to the riches of his grace." The ultimate hope for Germany and for all people is the redemption given us in Jesus Christ. Bonhoeffer never lost sight of that.

On June 8, with no reference to the Allied invasion, Bonhoeffer's mind is continuing to develop the thoughts of a worldly Christianity, a following of Christ *into the world*. The world since the Renaissance—and especially the Enlightenment—has been trying very hard to push Jesus Christ out of the way. The dominant worldview has come to be centered on human autonomy:

> The movement toward human autonomy (by which I mean discovery of the laws by which the world lives and manages its affairs in science, in society and government, in art, ethics, and religion), which began around the thirteenth century (I don't want to get involved in disputing exactly when), has reached a certain completeness in our

age. Human beings have learned to manage all important issues by themselves, without recourse to "Working hypothesis: God" (*DBWE* 8:425).

Science clearly has its limits. No scientist (I hope) goes home after a day in the lab and says to his wife, "Your pheromones are triggering an automatic response in me." He would be far better off saying, "You're beautiful, dear." The point, of course, is simply that we do not conduct the most important affairs of life in a scientific way. It was science that did the astounding work of unleashing atomic energy but it was other human factors that motivated us to create and use such a horrendous weapon. The problem with hatred is not that it is unscientific but that it is evil.

Love, joy, peace. These are not just gaps which science has not yet covered; they are realities of a far different nature than science.

Conservative Christians have been slow, however, to realize just how amazing modern science truly is. It frustrates me that science has been able to advance no substantial theory on what the "mind" is but that doesn't stop me from marveling at how much science has discovered about the brain. And no one can help but be greatly impressed at how much knowledge of DNA scientists have unraveled. It was science, not prayer, that eradicated polio. And, in genuine humility, we Christians must admit that, had the world not broken away from the strictures of the church, our scientific knowledge would be far less today.

What we in the church need to do is just what Bonhoeffer is calling for: an understanding of God in the midst of human life, human power and human achievement. That does not mean we forget the severe limitations on science but it does mean that we cease to think of science and faith as antagonists.

A good friend of mine was a scientist studying the DNA of plants. He worked with what I find to be unimaginably minute details. He awoke early each morning and found his mind and heart turning quickly to the Lord. Before even arising, he was praying, "Lord, what will you show me this morning? Will you help me to see a bit more about how your mind has worked in creation?" His prayer life did not supplant his use of the electron microscope and his lab work did not diminish his prayer life. The two were seamlessly part of his love of God. His work each day was an extended prayer for God to reveal himself in the structures of life.

And he hadn't even read Bonhoeffer! When he did discover Bonhoeffer, he found no trouble in recognizing what Bonhoeffer meant by finding God in the center, not at the fringes. That's what my friend had been doing all along. He was far from alone. When I was in campus ministry, I regularly visited more than two dozen university faculty members. One was in the English department, three were in engineering, and the rest were in the physical sciences. All were open followers of Jesus Christ and none saw any tension between his work and his faith. I talked with others in campus ministry at different universities. All reported the same thing: Most of the openly Christian professors they knew were scientists.

There simply is no opposition between science and faith until someone decides to use one of them to dominate the other. When Bible students claim that the earth is 6,000 years old (created in the autumn of 4004 B.C.!), they are creating a needless conflict. Genesis tells us who created the earth; science tells us how.

Bonhoeffer observes that the more the church tries to claim priority over science—rather than a partnership—the more anti-Christian the secular world becomes (*DBWE* 8:426). We create our own enemies!

"I consider the attack by Christian apologetics on the world's coming of age," Bonhoeffer wrote, "as, first of all, pointless, second, ignoble, and third, unchristian" (*DBWE* 8:427). It is a wrong-headed attack, unworthy of the children of the Creator, and quite unlike the Spirit of Jesus Christ.

Part of the problem, I am convinced, is that the unquestioning mind tends to easily become too defensive. It is wonderful to stay true to our roots in Scripture and devotion to Christ but it's a pitiful thing when we end up defending every belief we held yesterday. Until we are convinced that we know all the fullness of the mind of God, we had better be eager to learn, to grow, to change. That requires, of course, a great deal of unlearning. All learning is a process of disillusionment, a long train of discarded misunderstandings. That is normal in the process of growing up. It is marked by a spirit of humility and by a sense of security in our Lord, *not in our doctrine*. Or, as Bonhoeffer learned to word the matter, we are engaged with the real, living, present Jesus Christ, not merely with phraseological trappings.[19]

Where did we come up with the strategy of shaping evangelism around people's perceived needs? American history provides part of the answer. The First and especially the Second Great Awakenings (early eighteenth and early nineteenth century, respectively) were times in which personal guilt seemed to be a driving force in the fervor of the evangelistic meetings. The First was not planned but the Second, spearheaded to a large degree by Charles Finney, was very deliberate in its attempt to increase people's sense of guilt and need, then preach a Gospel of salvation as a relief, a cure. Often, in our defensive way, we have defended the practice so thoroughly that we have forgotten that evangelism can take a great many forms without ever having to make people feel badly before helping them feel better.[20]

Let's look at the phrase "the world come of age." This is important to Bonhoeffer. He had introduced the idea—without actually using the phrase—in *Ethics* (*DBWE* 6:120) when he spoke of nationalism emerging out of the French Revolution under the people's demand that the government was accountable to the people. The United States had recently formed a government with that sense of accountability but we were still too small to matter much. It was the French Revolution which brought the idea into the mainstream of Western thinking.

We use the phrase "come of age" to refer to a person who reaches the age of accountability, however much that age may differ from culture to culture. It doesn't mean the person has suddenly become virtuous but only that the person can no longer blame others for his or her weaknesses or problems. Those who have come of age are those who are held accountable for themselves, for their own character and their own decisions.

The "world come of age," likewise, does not mean the world had become virtuous in Bonhoeffer's lifetime. After all, he sits imprisoned by an unjust government. It means that the basic attitude that is coming to dominate the world is that we are responsible for ourselves. We are no longer children hiding behind the skirts of our mothers. We are no longer even under God's tutelage, to use a term impressed on Bonhoeffer especially by the Enlightenment philosopher Kant.[21] On the whole, we humans no longer "need" God to make sense of the world or of life. We can both explain them to a high degree and take responsibility for our own decisions within it.

I cannot think of a more perfect illustration of the "world come of age" than Michelangelo's magnificent statue of *David*. It was created in 1501-1504, commissioned by the city of Florence. Whatever may have been the original intention, the statue quickly came to be seen as an expression of Florentine greatness. The rock in David's right hand and the sling draped over his left shoulder make it clear that this is meant to be the biblical David, conqueror of the mighty giant Goliath.

This David, however, is no mere boy but a strong and extremely fit young man. There is nothing about the statue to suggest David's faith is centered anywhere but in his own strength. Even its size at seventeen feet conveys the undeniable power of David. Michelangelo's *David* embodies the world come of age, dependent not on God but on human power and potential.[22]

In our society there are numerous signs that Bonhoeffer was quite correct in his assessment. Books against God are best-sellers. Letters to newspaper editors routinely remind Christians that they should not "impose their religious views" on people by taking part in public discussions, since we live in a land marked by a separation of church and state. The world is confident it can get along just fine without God.

The response of the church to the world come of age has too often been to try harder to convince people that we really are weak and needy. Bonhoeffer, to the contrary, insists that we are to proclaim God not at the weak and needy fringes of life but at the middle, the strong points. We are not to fight against the world coming of age by trying to remind the world that we are a weak and feeble people. We are to be offering comfort to those who are hurting but thanksgiving on behalf of those who are in the midst of great blessing. It is common courtesy, not some abstract theological miscellany.

Bonhoeffer now switches gears a bit and comments that "the weakness of liberal theology was that it allowed the world the right to assign to Christ his place within it" (*DBWE* 8:428). Biologist Stephen Jay Gould expressed the Enlightenment idea of a strict separation between the realms of science and faith by speaking of "nonoverlapping magisteria."[23] Dominant in the West for more than two centuries has been the idea that faith is personal and private, while science and reason are the only permissible participants in the public forum. Christ is set aside, allowed only a minor role, usually at the time of weddings and funerals.

Eugene Peterson dwells on the same theme when he writes:

> All [our culture] asks is that I accept its definition of my work as an encourager of the culture's good will, as the priest who will sprinkle holy water on the culture's good intentions. . . . But if I, even for a moment, accept my culture's definition of me [as a pastor], I am rendered harmless. I can denounce evil and stupidity all I wish and will be tolerated in my denunciations as a court jester is tolerated.[24]

On July 8 Bonhoeffer picks up these themes again, commenting that we Christians have tended to accept our assigned role as outsiders to public affairs. We've been told that our faith, since it is irrational, must be merely private and inner. Bonhoeffer wants nothing of this:

> What I'm driving at is that God should not be smuggled in somewhere, in the very last, secret place that is left. Instead, one must simply recognize that the world and humankind have come of age. One must not find fault with people in their worldliness but rather confront them with God where they are strongest (*DBWE* 8:457).

We are not to seek areas where science and human management of life have not yet made much progress, then try to tell people that's where they'll find God. Instead, we are to stand in the middle of human achievement and proclaim in a non-religious way that Jesus Christ is Lord of all.

If we believe that Jesus Christ truly is the Lord of all, then—among other matters—there is absolutely no excuse for us not to be at the very forefront of the environmental movement. Human abuse of creation has clearly become a threat to the planet which our Lord has entrusted to us. Yet all too often, we see abuses of stewardship in the name of prospering the economy or refusing to acknowledge scientific evidence calling us towards becoming better stewards altogether. Such selfishness and short-sidedness are a terrible affront to the Creator and an awful rejection of our responsibility.

July 16 finds Bonhoeffer contemplating that earlier writers such as Hugo Grotius (1583-1645) had been on the right track in suggesting that we must live *etsi deus non daretur*, "as if there were no God." This is just another way of expressing the insights about non-religious or worldly Christianity. The world is learning to live that way and the followers of Christ are not to be resisting.

For Grotius, a jurist and amateur theologian, this idea was part of his Arminian theology, in which God's predestination of our lives does not dominate every decision we make. We are responsible for our own decisions and for shaping our own lives. A century later the "living-as-if-there-were-no-God" idea dovetailed nicely with Deism, which conceived the world as having been created by God and then set loose to follow natural laws.

For Bonhoeffer, however, this is simply biblical theology.[25] To see that, we need to be careful to see the context in which Bonhoeffer uses the phrase:

> The same God who makes us to live in the world without the working hypothesis of God is the God before whom we stand continually. Before God, and with God, we live without God" (*DBWE* 8:534).

In other words, it is *God's* choice that we live in full responsibility for our own choices. This is not a rebellion against God, not a rejection of the Lordship of Jesus Christ. It is simply a mature responsibility of the sort that every parent—including God!—wants for his or her children.

Those who cannot acknowledge that we live *as if* there were no God, making our own decisions and taking responsibility for our own lives, are unable to stand with non-believing humans, who live that way all the time. We only know how to relate to them when they weaken and falter. Wanting God to be above all the need-filler, we sit like vultures in the trees surrounding our culture, waiting for someone to collapse in weakness so we can swoop in and prey upon them. Not seeing that we ourselves live day by day as if there were no God, we are bothered to see others live that way, especially if they are doing well at it.

What is difficult for us is to sustain balance in our view of ourselves and of others. On the one hand, we cannot forget that "all have sinned and fall short of the glory of God" (Romans 3:23). Yet it is also true that we have been created in the image of God and therefore deserve to be treated with an extraordinary degree of respect and appreciation. Religious conservatives emphasize the first—our need for salvation—while progressives tend to emphasize the second—our God-given dignity. One way to describe what Bonhoeffer was seeking to do is to say he wanted to give full and equal weight to both of the seemingly opposite views of humankind.

We recall that he said in his May 5 letter that the center of everything is not our salvation but God's righteousness and kingdom. It is essential for understanding the whole book of Romans and the whole theology of Paul that when Paul speaks of righteousness he is thinking both of that quality which characterizes God *and* the righteousness which we ourselves receive as a gift of God's grace.

Perhaps Bonhoeffer failed to give proper weight to our justification while we evangelicals have paid far too little attention to the righteousness, the justice of God. Our neglect has allowed us to excuse ourselves from much of the struggle for social justice which has become a significant dimension of our society today. We take "righteousness" to be a personal, individual gift from God and dismiss "justice" as being something entirely distinct and relatively unimportant. That is a serious distortion of Scripture on our part. God expects righteousness *and* justice of us and does not even distinguish between the two. The Bible doesn't even have separate words for the two.[26]

Also in this letter:

> God consents to be pushed out of the world and onto the cross; God is weak and powerless in the world and in precisely this way, and only so, is at our side and helps us. Matthew 8:17[27] makes it quite clear that Christ helps us not by virtue of his omnipotence but rather by virtue of his weakness and suffering! This is the crucial distinction between Christianity and all religions. Human religiosity directs people in need to the power of God in the world. God as deus ex machina. The Bible directs people toward the powerlessness and the suffering of God; only the suffering God can help (*DBWE* 8:479).

Even as he calls people to solidarity with the world at the point of their strengths, Bonhoeffer calls us to solidarity with God at the point of his suffering and weakness. We cannot escape the fact that the Gospel was made real by the crucifixion and empty tomb of Jesus

Christ. Without the suffering of God as he accepted into himself the guilt and the consequence of our sin, we would have no reconciliation with God. Yes, the empty tomb meant that God overcame the utter helplessness of humankind in the face of death but there would have been no resurrection without the crucifixion. To seek to move from God's strength to human strength, bypassing the suffering of the cross, is to exclude ourselves from the meaning of the cross altogether. It is a form of triumphalism which Paul is always careful to avoid. The boldness of "I can do all things through him who strengthens me" is carefully balanced by "I have learned to be content with whatever I have" (Philippians 4:11-13).

He is keeping in tension two seemingly opposite movements, toward the suffering of God and toward the strength of humankind. How does he bring the two together? Perhaps he is thinking that Michelangelo's *David* is just a bluff. *David* is filled with confidence and power but of course there will always be a bigger giant awaiting us.

On July 18 Bonhoeffer returned to the themes he had left hanging in his previous letter. He reminded Bethge of a poem he had written not long before called "Christians and Heathens" (*DBWE* 8:460):

> People go to God when they're in need,
> plead for help, pray for blessing and bread,
> for rescue from their sickness, guilt, and death.
> So do they all, all of them, Christians and heathens.

> People go to God when God's in need,
> find God poor, reviled, without shelter or bread,
> see God devoured by sin, weakness, and death.
> Christians stand by God in God's own pain.

> God goes to all people in their need,
> fills body and soul with God's own bread,
> goes for Christians and heathens to Calvary's death
> and forgives them both.

A brief poem is not a sufficient ground on which to establish a conversation about universalism. Is Bonhoeffer suggesting that ultimately everyone is saved by the blood of Christ? That is not the important question to be raised by these few lines. What is striking is the middle verse about people discovering God in his weakness. Christians, he says, are those who do not turn away but stand by God at the very point of his pain.

That sounds almost bizarre to evangelical ears, in part because we have tended to pay little heed to those biblical passages which teach just what Bonhoeffer has in mind. Jesus, for example, told a parable about the glorious coming of the Son of Man who will gather to himself all those who have been blessed by his Father. Who are they? It is those who fed him when he was hungry, gave him drink when he thirsted, welcomed him when he was a stranger, clothed him when he was naked, cared for him in illness, visited him in prison (Matthew 25:35-36). To minister to the weak and needy is to minister to Jesus Christ, because he has identified with those very people. It takes no great dose of humility to admit, in fact, that we ourselves are numbered among the poor and needy. How many times has Jesus Christ walked into our churches, shabby and smelly, and been spurned?

Even more powerful is the realization that the greatest love, the greatest beauty, the greatest glory of God was seen in the immeasurable selflessness of the cross. To turn from God in his pain and suffering is to turn from the cross. And without the cross there is no empty tomb. We are not just to stand by God in his suffering but to take up our own cross and walk with Jesus Christ to that great moment of weakness on Calvary.[28] If we are to walk with Jesus, we are to walk with him on his own path, the *via dolorosa* to the cross.

Bonhoeffer builds on the idea of sharing in God's pain by reminding us that it is *in the world* that God suffers. It is at the hands of men and women that he accepts the pain we inflict on him:

> Being Christian . . . means being human, not a certain type of human being, but the human being Christ creates in us. It is not a religious act that makes someone a Christian but rather sharing in God's suffering in the worldly life (*DBWE* 8:480).

Martin Luther, according to a familiar legend, said that the mark of a Christian cobbler is not a cross emblazoned on every shoe, but simply a good shoe. May I confess a quirk of mine? I find few stores as depressing as Christian bookstores, filled with Jesus visors, Jesus pencils, Jesus shoelaces, Jesus stickers, and a hundred books on how to get more blessings from God. I try to imagine Jesus walking into such a store and all I can see is a dozen tables and bookshelves being thrown over.

A follower of Jesus, Bonhoeffer insists, is marked not by religious trappings but by worldliness, not by distinguishing himself or herself from the world but by solidarity with the world at the point of its strength and at the point of its pain. That is, the follower of Jesus is found where Jesus is.

The July 21 letter expanded on these ideas. We might find ourselves first skimming the letter to look for some reference to the failed assassination attempt of the day before. We find nothing and wonder if Bonhoeffer had even heard. My assumption is that he knew of it but dared not write a word of it, fearing that anything he might say could give a clue about his approval or even his participation:

> In the last few years I have come to know and understand more and more the profound this-worldliness of Christianity. The Christian is not a homo religiosus but simply a human being, in the same way that Jesus was a human being—in contrast, perhaps, to John the Baptist. I do not mean the shallow and banal this-worldliness of the enlightened, the bustling, the comfortable, or the lascivious, but the profound this-worldliness that shows discipline and includes the ever-present knowledge of death and resurrection (*DBWE* 8:485).

His mind at this point goes back to his first time in New York and a conversation he had with Jean Lasserre:

> I remember a conversation I had thirteen years ago in America with a young French pastor. We had simply asked ourselves what we really wanted to do with our lives. And he said, I want to become a saint (and I think it's possible that he did become one). This impressed me very much at the time. Nevertheless, I disagreed with him, saying something like: I want to learn to have faith. For a long time I did not understand the depth of this antithesis. I thought I myself could learn to have faith by trying to live something like a saintly life. I suppose I wrote Discipleship at the end of this path. Today I clearly see the dangers of that book, though I still stand by it (*DBWE* 8:485f).

There are two thoughts here which we must notice. One, of course, is that he looks back and sees some dangers in his earlier book.

(See Chapter Four for a discussion of these dangers.) Second, in this context, what demands our attention is his memory of the conversation with Jean Lasserre, unnamed but unmistakable in this context. Lasserre had spoken of hoping to become a saint. He was sincere in his devotion to Christ—as the rest of his life demonstrated—but a bit idealistic. We cannot make anything of ourselves at all.

Perhaps the two greatest enemies of the church, and especially of Christian leadership, are ambition and power. Often, of course, they are combined: a person is ambitious to gain power. Henri Nouwen, the Catholic priest who resonated so well with evangelicals, noted that Christian leadership "is not a leadership of power and control" but of "powerlessness and humility. . . . I am speaking of a leadership in which power is constantly abandoned in favor of love."[29]

Bonhoeffer remembers from that conversation that he had said something about wanting nothing more than to learn to have faith. And that's where he finds himself thirteen years later, still growing in faith.

Bonhoeffer goes on to express again his conviction that the followers of Jesus are to walk with him into the world, not retreat into a protective, self-imposed enclave:

> Later on I discovered, and am still discovering to this day, that one only learns to have faith by living in the full this-worldliness of life. If one has completely renounced making something of oneself—whether it be a saint or a converted sinner or a church leader (a so-called priestly figure!), a just or an unjust person, a sick or a healthy person—then one throws oneself completely into the arms of God and this is what I call this-worldliness: living fully in the midst of life's tasks, question, successes and failures, experiences, and perplexities—then one takes seriously no longer one's own sufferings but rather the suffering of God in the world. Then one stays awake with Christ in Gethsemane. And I think this is faith, this is metanoia. And this is how one becomes a human being, a Christian (Cf Jer 45!) How should one become arrogant over successes or shaken by one's failures when one shares in God's suffering in the life of this world? (*DBWE* 8:486).

Jeremiah 45 was often cited by Bonhoeffer, especially the thought in verse 6, which reads in part, "And you, do you seek great things for yourself? Do not seek them. . . ." Having had countless people all his life tell him how extraordinary he was, Bonhoeffer was always aware of the temptation to accept their adulation and begin thinking himself great. He resisted the temptation as diligently as he could but seems to have found at last the antidote. Living fully in this world, identifying with people whether they know God or not, busying oneself in "life's tasks, questions, successes and failures, experiences, and perplexities" protects one from focusing on his or her own sufferings.

This solidarity with the world does not mean that we lose ourselves in the world. When we open ourselves to the world in the sense Bonhoeffer has in mind, we find ourselves drawing closer to God, to the suffering of God in the world. We walk into the world, not without Christ, not leaving him behind in some sort of religious way station, but following Christ. We live in the world not *despite* our faith but *because* of it.

The difficulty, we might say, is in learning what Jesus meant when he prayed:

> They are not of the world, just as I am not of the world. Sanctify them in the truth; your word is truth. As you sent me into the world, so I have sent them into the world (John 17:16-18).

In the world but not of the world. Sent into the world, deliberately and directly but not dominated by the world. To the Romans Paul writes that we are not to be "conformed to this world" but are to be "transformed by the renewing of your minds, so that you may discern what is the will of God—what is good and acceptable and perfect" (Romans 12:2). The word here translated "conformed" is more literally "schematized." We are not to be pressed into a worldly scheme, a worldly set of priorities and values, a worldly mindset. Eugene Peterson suggests that we deal with the tension between being in the world but not of it, by remembering God's priorities for us:

> The grand essentials for me are immersion in Scripture and pursuit of prayer. We're not supposed to be dealing with the culture. We're supposed to be dealing with God. . . . I'm not saying we should close our eyes to the culture, but we don't need to study it that much. What the culture's doing is pretty shallow and stupid most of the time, and pretty obvious.[30]

We dwell in the world but we are not to forget our foundations in Bible and prayer. This decidedly does not mean that we hold onto religion but that we stand firmly on the solid ground of Scripture and of prayer. We live and move and have our being not in Christianity but in the doubly-spoken Word of God: Scripture and Jesus Christ.

Bonhoeffer might well protest here. It seems Peterson may be suggesting some sort of retreat from the world. Peterson would argue, I believe, that he is simply pointing out that what we need to know about culture in order to meaningfully relate to those around us is essentially unchanging. It is fascinating to see what electronic devices are doing to our young people but it is not of fundamental importance. More important are the 30,000- and 40,000-year-old hand prints on the walls of ancient caves. They are clear statements: I am here, I am somebody, I count. It takes no careful study of today's culture to understand that the human heart is besieged by the threats of loneliness, of not mattering to anyone, of not being loved. One of the points that I've heard Peterson make on numerous occasions is that, having watched enough TV news to have learned about three or four thousand murders, he doesn't need to learn of another. Nearly all of the news all of the time is mere repetition of yesterday's news.

Having said that, it remains a particular problem within evangelicalism that we have long since lost our understanding of how to engage the world in a significant way. That, in fact, is one of the most important reasons for studying Dietrich Bonhoeffer.

This letter of July 21, marking a time of profound change in Germany and in Bonhoeffer's situation, is the last of his letters to express substantial theological musings. When he writes the prayer—"May God lead us kindly through these times, but above all, may God lead us to himself"—it is as if he is pronouncing a benediction signaling the end of his own life.

Execution

Bonhoeffer had been transferred in October from Tegel prison to the Reich Central Security building on Prinz Albrecht Strasse and then on February 7, 1944, to the Buchenwald concentration camp. From there he was in a small group sent from Buchenwald on April 3, just days before it was liberated.

While the prisoners were on the road south, it must have occurred to Bonhoeffer that April 5 was the second anniversary of his arrest. What he would not have known was that on that very day Hitler ordered the immediate execution of all who were suspected of being part of the conspiracy. After a few days of travel, the truck load of prisoners arrived at the Flossenburg concentration camp, arriving on the Sunday after Easter, April 8, 1944.[31]

Some of the prisoners, including Vassily Kokorin, nephew of Soviet Foreign Minister Molotov, asked Bonhoeffer to lead them in a worship service. By a very striking coincidence, the lectionary text for the day was Isaiah 53:5, which reads, "With his stripes we are healed," and 1 Peter 1:3, which says, "Blessed be the God and Father of our Lord Jesus Christ. By his great mercy we have been born anew to a living hope through the resurrection of Jesus Christ from the dead."

Early in the morning of Monday, April 9, conspirators Wilhelm Canaris, Hans Oster, Dietrich Bonhoeffer, and others, were stripped of their clothes and hanged in a Flossenburg courtyard. Their bodies, now stripped even of the Spirit of Jesus Christ, were burned. The ashes were swept into a mound, still visible, now grassy, forever testifying to the immeasurable evil of the day, but reminding us too of the great and beautiful goodness which God planted in the hearts and souls of these sacrificial men.

Two weeks later, Flossenburg was liberated by the Allies. Another week after that, April 30, 1945, Hitler committed suicide. On May 7, Germany surrendered unconditionally, with the final documents of surrender signed in Berlin on May 8.

It was not until late July 1945 that Bonhoeffer's family and Maria learned of Dietrich's death. They had to accept also the executions of Dietrich's brother Klaus and two brothers-in-law, Rüdiger Schleicher and Hans von Dohnanyi.

Among Bonhoeffer's last words were spoken to a fellow prisoner: "This is the end but for me the beginning."

Endnotes

1   *DBWE* 8:486.

2   Schlingensiepen, 316.

3   It was not until late September 1944 that the Gestapo could prove that Bonhoeffer was involved in the conspiracy, though they had come to suspect it earlier. Hans von Dohnanyi, the key figure in the conspiracy, had been keeping careful

4   In a certain dark coincidence, at the time of the July 20 assassination attempt Bonhoeffer was reading Dostoevsky's *Memoirs from the House of the Dead*. In a July 25 letter to Bethge he mentions having finished the book and notes, "I am preoccupied with [Dostoevsky's] claim . . . that no person can live without hope." He then cites 1 Timothy 1:1, "Christ our hope. . . ."

(notes continued)

notes for several years on Nazi atrocities. He thought the notes would be of value in the trials that would follow the war but with an unusual carelessness on his part, he named the conspirators encoding their identities by using their initials. Once found, his notes became the final condemnation for the conspirators.

5   Catherine Drinker Bowen, *Francis Bacon: The Temper of a Man*, 109.

6   The battle against religion is not waged solely by those outside the church and is not a battle recently begun. John Stott quotes an ancient church father: "As Chrysostom [349-407] put it, the signs of Paul's apostolic priesthood were 'not the long garment and the bells as they of old, nor the mitre and the turban, but signs and wonders, far more aweful (*sic*) than these'" (Stott, *Romans*, 381). Centuries before that the prophets cried out against religion. See Amos 5:21-24 and Micah 6:6-8.

7   Walter Brueggemann, *Abiding Astonishment* (Louisville, Kentucky: Westminster/John Knox Press, 1991), 10.

8   Walter Brueggemann, *Interpretation and Obedience* (Minneapolis: Fortress Press, 1991), 43.

9   Emily Dickinson, Poem 1120.

10 Very likely a reference to the Marxist statement that religion is the opium of the people.

11 Herbert Butterfield, *Christianity, Diplomacy and War* (New York, Abingdon: Cokesbury Press) 4.

12 The "*deus ex machina*" in ancient Greek and Roman plays was a god-figure brought in to magically solve problems that humans couldn't. The figure would sometimes enter suspended from a cable, by a machine, for a more impressive effect. Bonhoeffer is suggesting that we often treat God this way, as the one who enters the scene only when we humans work ourselves into a jam from which we cannot extract ourselves. The old saying that "there are no atheists in fox holes" is suggestive of the same idea that we call on God only when we're faced with challenges beyond our resources.

13 Ole Hallesby, *Prayer* (Minneapolis: Augsburg, 1931, 1959), 11.

14 This is the title of an excellent short book by Bethge in which he explores the realities of the church which emerged from the war. He notes that there has been very little change. Bonhoeffer had written about prayer and righteous action in the sermon he would have delivered had he been free on the occasion of the baptism of Eberhard and Renate Bethge's child, Dietrich.

15 Eugene Peterson, *The Contemplative Pastor*, 51.

16 This is not as strange an idea as it may sound at first. In my own experience, one of the finest examples of Christlikeness of character was InterVarsity staff member Mary Beaton. She was very much present in the world and was in no way "other worldly." In this way, she very much reflected the character of God in the midst and not at the edges. There was no place in her thinking for "God the magician." She was a person of integrity, common sense, love, kindness, insight, and deep compassion. Colossians 3:1-17 is an excellent exposition of the idea that the "things above" are the relational terms "compassion, kindness, humility, meekness, and patience" (Colossians 3:12).

17 Anderson, Ray S., "Ten Theses on Dietrich Bonhoeffer: Theologian, Christian, Martyr," in *Theology News and Notes*, December, 2013.

18 Didn't someone once say that consistency is the hobgoblin of small minds? At one point Bonhoeffer can speak of our redemption as if it were a minor detail in the Gospel, while here he agrees with the Moravian devotional that it is the central message of the Gospel. Were we to ask him, I suspect he would simply say that the lordship of Jesus Christ and our redemption cannot be separated from one another. Jesus is simultaneously Lord *and* Savior.

19 At some point in prison, Bonhoeffer jotted down this note: "It is the advantage and the essence of the strong that they are able to pose the great decisive questions and take clear positions on them" (*DBWE* 8:494). Those who have answers without questions tend to be defensive and insecure.

20 The debate over whether humankind is essentially good or bad has been with us for many years. In the early fifteenth century Pope Innocent III wrote a small book entitled *On the Misery of Human Life*. A Christian humanist named Giannozzo Manetti responded with an essay entitled *On the Dignity of Man*, in which he argues that the pleasures of life outweigh the miseries and the goodness of people outweigh our dark side. Manetti based his position on the simple happiness of most people, on the writings of the old Roman sages, and especially on the Bible.

21 Kant wrote: "Enlightenment is man's release from his self-incurred tutelage. Tutelage is man's inability to make use of his understanding without direction from another. Self-incurred is the tutelage when its cause lies not in lack of reason but in lack of resolution and courage to use it without direction from another. *Sapere Aude!* 'Have courage to use your own reason!'—that is the motto of the enlightenment." Cited in Brown, *Christianity and Western Thought*, 285. For Bonhoeffer, the idea of outgrowing our time of tutelage was strengthened by the German historian Wilhelm Dilthey (*DB* 866f). Bonhoeffer's own maternal grandfather, church historian Karl August von Hase, had written against those who wanted German Lutheranism to remain in the exact mold of Luther's day by saying the world would no longer live within such dogmatic constraints because of "the already awakened reason of the people" (*DB* 6).

22 The opening image in Kenneth Clark's ground-breaking documentary series *Civilisation* (available on YouTube) is the head of Michelangelo's grand statue, as if this is the first place to look if one wants to see civilization at its best.

23 *Nature* magazine, March, 1997: 16ff.

24 Eugene Peterson, *The Contemplative Pastor*, 24.

25 Ray S. Anderson, *Practical Theology*, 17f., says Bonhoeffer's thinking here shows that he "was a forerunner of what later was to become the domain of practical theology. . . . Bonhoeffer laid the groundwork for a praxis-oriented theology through an ethic of discipleship and obedience, where theory emerges only through engagement with truth as an ethical demand in the form of the claim of Christ through the other person. In this sense also Bonhoeffer can be considered a forerunner of what has come to be known as postmodernism."

26 The Greek root is *dik-*. In its various inflections it can mean "right," "righteous," "righteousness," "just," "fair," "justice," or any other word in this family of ideas. It is broad in its scope when used to emphasize justice, it does not exclude righteousness or vice versa. Realizing that, biblically, righteousness and justice are in the same family of ideas will protect us from the modern distortion of thinking righteousness is personal virtue and justice is a social value that is none of the church's business.

27 Matthew 8:17 refers to Isaiah 53:4: "This was to fulfill what had been spoken through the prophet Isaiah, "He took our infirmities and bore our diseases."

28 Leonard Bernstein's Second Symphony, *Kaddish*, develops through poetry and music this theme of God's weakness. He ends up, however, seeming to portray us responding to God in strength. Bonhoeffer is more biblical, recognizing that we *share* God's weakness, even as at other times we share his strength. And Bonhoeffer is more biblical in seeing that God's strength is revealed in and through his weakness. Paul's comment, "When I am weak, then I am strong," applies both to Paul as a human follower of Jesus Christ *and to God himself.*

29 Henri Nouwen, *In the Name of Jesus* (New York: Crossroads, 1993), 63.

30 Eugene Peterson, "Return to the Timeless," *Leadership Journal*, Spring, 1991, 22.

31 The details which follow are those enumerated by Ferdinand Schlingensiepen, 278.

CHAPTER EIGHT

Conclusion

This noble example to his sheep he gave:
That first he did and then he taught.[1]

Let us go then, you and I,
When the evening is spread out against the sky
Like a patient etherised upon a table;
Let us go, through certain half-deserted streets,
The muttering retreats
Of restless nights in one-night cheap hotels
And sawdust restaurants with oystershells:
Streets that follow like a tedious argument
Of insidious intent
To lead you to an overwhelming question…
Oh, do not ask, "What is it?"
Let us go and make our visit.

Thus begins T. S. Eliot's poem, "The Love Song of J. Alfred Prufrock." Eliot knows, of course, that we cannot resist asking, What is it? What is the overwhelming question?

It is the question that can never quite be captured by words and can never be answered except by faith. Prufrock himself, later in the poem, comes close to the question when he asks, "Do I dare disturb the universe?" It is a bold question for one whose life is thoroughly enmeshed in the mundane. Prufrock says he has "measured out my life with coffee spoons."

Dietrich Bonhoeffer disturbed the universe. His feet were not enmeshed in the world of human convention but neither was he trying to rid himself of the world, to escape to some heavenly plane. His life is the fruit of Jesus' prayer that we might be in the world but not "of the world" (John 17:11-19). He was in the world and challenging its assumptions, just as he was in the church and challenging its ways.

Dietrich's half-deserted streets, the often lonely streets that led him to the edge of what can be known and understood, left him with his own ultimate question that continues to challenge us three quarters of a century later: *"Who is Jesus Christ actually for us today?"* (*DBWE* 8:362). He was not at all suggesting that each generation molds a new Jesus in its own image, though something like that seems common enough in the history of the church. Rather, his question was, How can we recognize Jesus in our own day and speak of Jesus in a way that can be heard and understood in our own generation? How are we to relate to Jesus Christ in our non-religious world come of age?

As we saw in Chapter Two, when called by God to return to Egypt and lead the Israelites to the Promised Land, Moses asks, "Who am I?" (Exodus 3:11). The Lord's answer is very instructive. The answer to the question, Who am I?, is in effect reformulated by God into a deeper question, to whom are you related? In what relationship is your identity? When we ask the Lord to identify us, he tells us we are not alone because he is with us. Bonhoeffer shows a great sensitivity to this, always calling us to recognize that we are who we are *only in our communion and identification with Jesus Christ* and thereby also with one another.

The first question he explored in his famous poem, "Who Am I?" (*DBWE* 8:459). He was experiencing what psychoanalyst Erik Erikson was calling at the time an "identity crisis."[2] For Bonhoeffer, there was only one resolution. The poem concludes, "Whoever I am, you know, O Lord, I am yours." All that was certain was his relationship with Jesus Christ. So the deeper question is not, Who am I?, but "Who are you, Lord?" Who, indeed, is Jesus Christ for us today?

As John Matthews reminds us so simply:

> What has historically given strength to God's faithful people during times of trauma and transition has not so much been what they held on to from the past, but rather who they looked to for their present and future.[3]

Bonhoeffer, as we have seen, pushes the matter still further. There is a third question. The first is, Who am I? The second and deeper question is, Who is Jesus Christ for us today? The third question seeks to understand the implications of the first two: How then shall we live?

How shall we live? We are to live "before God and with God as if there were no God"(*DBWE* 8:479, letter of July 16, 1944). That sounds shocking to us, mostly because we tend not to hear the first part. We are to live fully aware that we are in the presence of God. We are to live without forgetting that Jesus Christ is our life, that communion with him is the whole of life for us. Yet, Bonhoeffer says, there is a sense in which we live as if there were no God. What does he mean?

If we would be honest with ourselves, we would see that we already live that way. We make decisions by gathering the necessary information, taking our goals into consideration, and choosing the path that we want. We trust that God is leading and teaching us but very seldom do we have a direct sense that God wants us to do this deed or say that word. In nearly every situation we live by our own choices. There is nothing new about that, nothing out of the ordinary, and nothing displeasing to God.

Only little children need someone else to make all their decisions for them.

But what of all the guidance and teaching we have from God? What of Torah? Do we somehow outgrow that? Not at all. You may recall the observation in Chapter Four that there are three ways to live. We can submit to the rules, remaining good but essentially irresponsible children. Or we can break the rules, like rebellious adolescents. Or we can hear Torah, understand the direction of its call, and move beyond the letter. We can recognize freedom in moving beyond a "living by the rules" mentality as we learn to embrace living by the Spirit. We must remember the words inscribed in Dietrich's Bible: "The letter kills but the Spirit gives life" (2 Corinthians 3:6).

Again, John Matthews puts it succinctly:

> . . . the goal for those who are mature should be responsible interdependence . . . maturity would mean thinking, deciding, and acting responsibly, having grown beyond adolescent dependency on one's parent or tutor or God (!) for answers, permission, or detailed direction.[4]

The challenges facing the church today are not just those of finding ways for us to help one another grow into a mature faith. The cultural context in the West is in the midst of its most drastic change since the Renaissance. The world itself has come of age!

My favorite snapshot of the Renaissance is the *Oration on the Dignity of Man*, a 1486 essay by Pico della Mirandola. It captures the blossoming of a spirit of independence among Renaissance thinkers.

At one level they were experiencing an independence from the Roman church, which was unusually corrupt during this era. As we can see from the following paragraph, however, there is an underlying sense of independence from God. This is not a disbelief in God but rather a declaration that, while God may have been our Creator, we ourselves are the shapers of our own character. It is an early form of Deism, articulated as if by God himself:

> Neither a fixed abode nor a form that is thine alone nor any function peculiar to thyself have we given thee, Adam, to the end that according to thy longing and according to thy judgment thou mayest have and possess what abode, what form, and what functions thou thyself shalt desire. The nature of all other beings is limited and constrained with the bounds of laws prescribed by Us. Thou, constrained by no limits, in accordance with thine own free will, in whose hand We have placed thee, shalt ordain for thyself the limits of thy nature. We have set thee at the world's center that thou mayest from thence more easily observe whatever is in the world. We have made thee neither of heaven nor of earth, neither mortal nor immortal, so that with freedom of choice and with honor, as though the maker and molder of thyself, thou mayest fashion thyself in whatever shape thou shall prefer. Thou shalt have the power to degenerate into the lower forms of life, which are brutish. Thou shalt have the power, out of thy soul's judgment, to be reborn into the higher forms, which are divine.[5]

Contemplating this paragraph leads us to an interesting observation about Bonhoeffer. We know that he had little patience with the materialistic rationalism that emerged during the Enlightenment, but we can see here a certain similarity between the spirit of the Renaissance and Bonhoeffer's thought. Before God and with God, we live as though there were no God. Is this so far from what Pico said? We live as free, responsible adults *by God's choice and command*. We do not wrest our lives from God's control but simply exercise the responsibility he has entrusted to us.

The problem, of course, is that as the centuries have progressed our culture has let the pendulum swing so far that God has become excluded from the scene entirely.

"Western culture is founded on human autonomy," say Richard Middleton and Brian Walsh.[6] They note that John Dewey—the American philosopher, psychologist and educator—wrote in 1929 that the spirit of modern life is marked by four qualities:

1. No more preoccupation with the supernatural.
2. Growing belief in the power of individual minds.
3. Optimism about the unlimited future.
4. Patient and experimental study of nature as the only way forward.

Bonhoeffer may not have read Dewey, though he would certainly have heard of him while in America in 1930 and 1931. We do know that he read while in prison the writings of Wilhelm Dilthey, who argued that the West had been moving toward autonomy since the thirteenth century and that the Enlightenment was our time of arrival.[7]

One may look back on the twentieth century and wonder how the West maintained its certainty that the greatness of human reason guarantees a good future for the human race. The unsinkable Titanic sank. Two wars were so extensive that we call them "world wars," words which ought to catch in our throats. Millions were burned in gas chambers. We have made tens of thousands of bombs capable of such destructive force that we could destroy the human race in a few horrible minutes.

During the twentieth century our artists and poets could see through our adolescent sense of invincibility. In 1912 Duchamp painted *Nude Descending a Staircase*, portraying a robotic humanoid in descent. John Cage "wrote" a piece of music called "4' 33", which consists of nothing but silence. The Irish poet Yeats said, ". . . the center will not hold."[8] T. S. Eliot wrote:

> We are the hollow men
> We are the stuffed men
> Leaning together
> Headpiece filled with straw. Alas!
> Our dried voices, when
> We whisper together
> Are quiet and meaningless
> As wind in dry grass
> Or rats' feet over broken glass
> In our dry cellar

> Shape without form, shade without colour,
> Paralysed force, gesture without motion;
> Those who have crossed
> With direct eyes, to death's other Kingdom
> Remember us if at all not as lost
> Violent souls, but only
> As the hollow men
> The stuffed men.

Our artists are people of vision, seeing our reality and seeing right through it. Yes, in the twentieth century we finally achieved the power to make the words of Mirandola seem sensible. And in the twenty-first century we are exploring Artificial Intelligence, with some predicting that we'll be able to clone and even replace the human mind. Whether we are DuChamp's mechanical people or Eliot's hollow people, in any case we are arriving at our moment of greatest power and discovering we have somehow left our own humanity behind.

Yet, for better or worse, modern—and especially postmodern—culture has assumed responsibility for the shape of human life in our day. Bonhoeffer would not have us undo this step. We must not and we cannot go back to immaturity. The problem is that the center is hollow. We are lord of our own lives, breaking the complementarity which gives us our very identity. Christians want to live "before God and with God" but have little idea how to live "without God." Non-believers are trying to live without God but, by refusing to live "before God and with God," remain hollow.

Dietrich Bonhoeffer is helping us see how to be fully human, to live fully before God and with God and without God.

We read Bonhoeffer today only in part because of his insights into the theological issues of our time. We want to know Dietrich Bonhoeffer himself. His life gives credence to his work and his works express the integrity of his faith.

Who was this man, Dietrich Bonhoeffer? A faithful follower of Jesus Christ, that's what he might say as most defining of himself. We, of course, want to hear something more individual, something which accounts for his unique story and bold writing. When Bonhoeffer himself tried to give such an answer in his poem "Who Am I?", he had to settle for just this: "Whoever I am, you know me, O God. You know I am yours." May we learn to say as much of ourselves.

Endnotes

1. Chaucer, Geoffrey, *The Canterbury Tales*, lines 496-497.
2. As Bonhoeffer was asking these questions in a German prison, German-American psychoanalyst Erik Erikson was beginning to recognize that one of the most important questions of the day is, Who am I? Erickson, raised in the confusing world of Berlin but fleeing Germany in 1933, noted that western culture in the first half of the twentieth century was marked by a personal "identity crisis." Children were growing up with little or no sense of who they really were. See his highly influential *Childhood and Society* (New York: W. W. Norton Company, 1950).
3. John Matthews, *Anxious Souls Will Ask: The Christ-Centered Spirituality of Dietrich Bonhoeffer* (Grand Rapids: Wm. B. Eerdmans Publishing Co., 2005), 2.
4. Ibid., 31.
5. Werner L, Gundersheimer, ed., *The Italian Renaissance* (Toronto: University of Toronto Press, 1965), 96.
6. J. Richard Middleton and Brian J. Walsh, *Truth Is Stranger Than It Used To Be: Biblical Faith in a Post-Modern Age* (Madison, Wisconsin: InterVarsity Press, 1995).
7. John DeGruchy, in the introduction to *Letters and Papers from Prison*, vol. 8 of *DBWE*, 23.
8. Cited in Kenneth Clark, *Civilization* (New York: Harper and Row, 1969)

EPILOGUE

Germany after the War

It was frustrating for the conspirators that the Allies granted them no credibility. Through Bonhoeffer they had tried to convince the West, especially Churchill, that within an hour after the successful assassination of Hitler they would have the rudiments of a new government in place, fully cooperative with the Allies in ending the war immediately. Churchill would have none of it.

The front page of the military newspaper, *Stars and Stripes,* for Wednesday, May 2, 1945, gives a clear confirmation that Churchill was not unrealistic. Hitler was dead but Admiral Doenitz was quick to promise the war was not over. Churchill had long since decided that the war was not against Hitler alone but all of Germany, since support for the Führer had been so strong, widespread, and long-lasting.

In fact, however, Doenitz was bluffing. He knew full well that the war effort was hopeless for Germany. Mussolini, never a valuable ally for Germany, was executed on April 28. German forces in Italy surrendered on April 29. And on April 30 Adolf Hitler committed suicide, at last agreeing that the conspirators had been right all along: he needed to die. The Russians had already entered Berlin from one side and the British and American forces were just outside the city on the other.

Hitler had been driven near madness in the last few months as the inevitable outcome of the war became obvious even to him. His military orders became bizarre. He wanted the execution of Jews to be carried out as quickly as possible. On April 5 he ordered the deaths of any and all who had been even slightly suspected of involvement in the conspiracy. Dietrich Bonhoeffer, his brother, and two brothers-in-law were killed just three weeks before Hitler's suicide.

So Doenitz' bluff was brief. Unconditional surrender papers were signed in France on May 7 and in Berlin on May 8, 1945.

Dietrich's twin sister Sabine and her husband, long exiled in England, were not able to return to Germany until the summer of 1947. A boat across the channel, a train through Brussels and into Germany, and they were in the now-strange land they called home. The first German words they heard on crossing the border into Aachen were spoken by a worker at the station: "Karl, where have you put the lamp?"[1] That was the perfect question in post-war Germany. Where indeed was the light on the path into the future?

Now came the time of reconstruction in Europe, even while the Pacific War continued for another few months. Bonhoeffer had been thinking of and preparing for the post-War period for several years. Among other thoughts on his mind, Dietrich had even included in *Ethics* something of a "sample" confession which he hoped the church would make after being freed from Hitler's stranglehold.

That confession on behalf of the church begins on page 137 of *DBWE* 8 and is very extensive. The boldest words are these:

> The church confesses that it has not professed openly and clearly enough its message of the one God, revealed for all times in Jesus Christ and tolerating no other gods besides. The church confesses its timidity, its deviations, its dangerous concessions. It has often disavowed its duties as sentinel and comforter. Through this it has often withheld the compassion that its owes to the despised and rejected. The church was mute when it should have cried out, because the blood of the innocent cried out to heaven. The church did not find the right word in the right way at the right time. It did not resist to the death the falling away from faith and is guilty of the godlessness of the masses.
>
> The church confesses that it has misused the name of Christ by being ashamed of it before the world and by not

resisting strongly enough the misuse of that name for evil ends. The church has looked on while the injustice and violence have been done, under the cover of the name of Christ. It has even allowed the most holy name to be openly derided without contradiction and has thus encouraged that derision. The church recognizes that God will not leave unpunished those who so misuse God's name as it does.

The church confesses that it has witnessed the arbitrary use of brutal force, the suffering in body and soul of countless innocent people, that it has witnessed oppression, hatred, and murder without raising its voice for the victims and without finding ways of rushing to help them. It has become guilty of the lives of the weakest and most defenseless brothers and sisters of Jesus Christ.

The church confesses its guilt toward the countless people whose lives have been destroyed by slander, denunciation, and defamation. It has not condemned the slanderers for their wrongs and has thereby left the slandered to their fate.

The church confesses that it has coveted security, tranquillity, peace, property, and honor to which it has no claim, and therefore has not bridled human covetousness, but promoted it (*DBWE* 8:137f).

Events soon proved that Bonhoeffer's hope was in vain. The church in Germany did not emerge from the Hitler years with a sense of repentance and renewed devotion to Jesus Christ. Bethge points out a symbol of the church's failure to repent: When a rebuilt church in the Moabit district of Berlin was dedicated, Berlin's Mayor Reuter drove up in a Volkswagen while Bishop Dibelius arrived in a Mercedes. Bethge notes simply, "And the people in Moabit noticed that at once."[2] The church had failed to relinquish its sense of privilege and status, had failed to become a servant to the people. Bonhoeffer would have been deeply offended.

Even before this, however, the church in Germany had shown its pale colors. On October 19, 1945, the church had issued a "Declaration of Guilt" in Stuttgart. It was put forth reluctantly, at the insistence of Western church leaders who sought an ecumenical restoration of mutual trust and respect between the German churches and others. And it was too weak to be called a real confession.

As they had been at the end of World War I, the Germans were simply unable to accept responsibility for the horrors they had instigated. The church offered no leadership whatsoever in helping the people experience a genuine repentance.

The church's "repentance" was feeble at best, more likely simply disingenuous:

> We are all the more grateful for this visit [from Western church leaders], as we not only know that we are with our people in a large community of suffering, but also in a solidarity of guilt.
>
> With great pain we say: By us infinite wrong was brought over many peoples and countries. That which we often testified to in our communities, we express now in the name of the whole church: We did fight for long years in the name of Jesus Christ against the mentality that found its awful expression in the National Socialist regime of violence; but we accuse ourselves for not standing to our beliefs more courageously, for not praying more faithfully, for not believing more joyously, and for not loving more ardently.
>
> Now a new beginning is to be made in our churches. Based on the Holy Scripture, with complete seriousness directed to the lord of the church, they start to cleanse themselves of the influences of beliefs foreign to the faith and to reorganize themselves. We hope to the God of grace and mercy that He will use our churches as His tools and give them licence to proclaim His word and to obtain obedience for His will, amongst ourselves and among our whole people.
>
> The fact that we, in this new beginning, find ourselves sincerely connected with the other churches of the ecumenical community fills us with great joy.
>
> We hope to God that by the common service of the churches the spirit of violence and revenge, which today again wants to become powerful, will be directed to the whole world,

and that the spirit of peace and love comes to predominate, in which alone tortured humanity can find healing.

Thus we ask at a time, in which the whole world needs a new beginning: *Veni creator Spiritus!*"[3]

The false claim that "We did fight for long years in the name of Jesus Christ against the mentality that found its awful expression in the National Socialist regime of violence" completely eviscerates the small hint of repentance expressed in the rest of the document. For two of the signatories—Martin Niemoller and Hans Asmussen—the claim was true but for the church at large it was not even a rough approximation of the reality.

Furthermore, weak as it was, the Declaration was resented by many Germans in the years after the war. Victoria Barnett quotes one German expressing what many felt: "Because—most people believed this—the occupation troops were responsible for the misery. 'They're just as inhuman as we were,' was how it was put. And with that, everything was evened up."[4]

Were Bonhoeffer and the other conspirators considered heroes once Hitler was out of the way? Not at all. Most in Germany considered them to have betrayed the nation. Even Bonhoeffer's own church in Brandenburg denounced the conspiracy (*DB* 931). Biographer Ferdinand Schlingensiepen tells us that for many years after the war there remained a strong sense that those who had opposed Hitler had been traitors against Germany:

> Commemorations of the attempted overthrow on 20 July 1944 had been held since 1946 but were still an embarrassment to many politicians in 1967. Adenauer [German Chancellor from 1949 to 1963], though he had been consistently opposed to Hitler, never attended these ceremonies. He knew how unpopular it would have been for him as chancellor to do so.[5]

Westerners may have difficulty understanding how the Germans could acknowledge that Hitler had been evil and that, in their inadequate resistance, they had fostered the spread of that evil, yet still believe that the duty of a good German was to obey. It is insufficient to say merely that the Germans had an unusually strong sense of national pride. Their deep-seated pride was not precisely in Germany as a political entity but in the *Volk*, the Germanic people whose strength had been legendary at least as far back as their repulsion of the mighty Roman armies almost twenty centuries earlier.

This pride in and devotion to the *Volk* hindered even the most ardent of resistors, up to and including Bonhoeffer. It helps to explain, for example, why the Confessing Church began primarily as a defense against Hitler's interference with the church, not so much a resistance against all Hitler was doing in Germany. And it helps to explain why the conspirators wanted so badly to have the Allies ready to recognize the new German state as soon as Hitler was dead. They were sure the West would recognize that the *Volk* were basically good and trustworthy despite their momentary distraction by Hitler.

One of the great hindrances to the freedom of pastors to join the Confessing Church had been the fact that the evangelical church (i.e., Lutheran, Reformed, and United) was supported by tax monies collected by the national government. Joining the Confessing Church meant surrendering one's right to a government salary and becoming dependent on the freewill offerings of the congregations, a most precarious position in a country in deep financial difficulty. Most odd from our perspective is that the system has been modified but not discarded in today's Germany.

It is a centuries-old tradition that the state has favored religion, usually just one amongst others, as a socially stabilizing force in society. That works well until the time comes that people of faith, in obedience to the Lord of justice, must speak out and even act against the state. As Bonhoeffer and many others learned, sometimes one must jam the wheels of state with one's own body.

In the end, both Bonhoeffer and Hitler died but that does not mean they ended up with the same fate. Today we use Hitler's name as synonymous with evil, while decades of reflection are causing people around the globe to honor the memory of Dietrich Bonhoeffer and his colleagues.

Geoffrey Chaucer lived five centuries before Bonhoeffer, during a period when the church was deeply corrupt. Chaucer saw—or imagined—one lowly, local pastor who was an exception. The description of that fourteenth century pastor fits Dietrich Bonhoeffer. Alongside Chaucer's delightful words I've appended my own translation, trying to capture the flavor but not pretending to match the genius of Chaucer.

A good man was ther of religioun,	A good man there was of religion;
And was a povre Persoun of a Toun,	He was a poor Parson of a town
But riche he was of hooly thought and werk.	But rich he was in holy thought and work.
He was also a lerned man, a clerk,	He was also a learned man, a student,
That Cristes gospel trewely wolde preche;	That Christ's Gospel truly would preach;
his parisshens devoutly wolde he teche.	His parishioners devoutly would he teach.
Benygne he was, and wonder diligent,	Benign he was, and wonderfully diligent,
And in adveresitee ful pacient,	And in adversity fully patient,
And swich he was ypreved ofte sithes,	As such he was often proven.
Full looth were hym to cursen for his tithes,	Fully loath he was to curse for his income,
but rather wolde he yeven, out of doute,	But instead he would give, without a doubt,
Unto his povre parisshens aboute of his offryng and eek of his substaunce.	Unto his poor parishioners 'round about, From his offerings and also his substance.
He koude in litel thyng have suffisaunce.	He could in little things have sufficience.
Wyd was his parisshe, and houses fer asonder,	Wide was his parish, with houses far asunder;
but he ne lefte nat, for reyn ne thonder,	But he never neglected—even for rain or thunder,
In siknesse nor in meschief to visite	Nor in sickness or in mischief— to visit
The ferreste in his parisshe, muche and lite,	The farthest in his parish, great and small,
Upon his feet, and in his hand a staf.	He walked it all, with a staff in his hand.
A good man was ther of religioun,	A good man there was of religion;
And was a povre Persoun of a Toun,	He was a poor Parson of a town
But riche he was of hooly thought and werk.	But rich he was in holy thought and work.
He was also a lerned man, a clerk,	He was also a learned man, a student,

That Cristes gospel trewely
  wolde preche;
his parisshens devoutly wolde he
  teche.
Benygne he was, and wonder
  diligent,
And in adveresitee ful pacient,
And swich he was ypreved ofte
  sithes,
Full looth were hym to cursen for
  his tithes,
but rather wolde he yeven, out of
  doute,
Unto his povre parisshens aboute
 of his offryng and eek of his
  substaunce.
He koude in litel thyng have
  suffisaunce.
Wyd was his parisshe, and
  houses fer asonder,
but he ne lefte nat, for reyn ne
  thonder,
In siknesse nor in meschief to
  visite
The ferreste in his parisshe,
  muche and lite,
Upon his feet, and in his hand a
  staf.
This nobble ensample to his
  sheep he yaf,
That first he wroghte, and
  afterward he taughte.
Out of the gospel he tho wordes
  caughte,
And this figure he added eek
  therto,
That if gold ruste, what shal iron
  do?
For if a preest be foul, on whom
  we truste,
No wonder is a dewed man to
  ruste;

His parishioners devoutly would
  he teach.
Benign he was, and wonderfully
  diligent,
And in adversity fully patient,
As such he was often proven.
Fully loath he was to curse for
  his income,
But instead he would give,
  without a doubt,
Unto his poor parishioners
  'round about,
From his offerings and also his
  substance.
He could in little things have
  sufficience.
Wide was his parish, with
  houses far asunder;
But he never neglected—even
  for rain or thunder,
Nor in sickness or in mischief—
  to visit
The farthest in his parish, great
  and small,
He walked it all, with a staff in
  his hand.
This noble example to his sheep
  he gave:
That first he did and then he
  taught.
Out of the gospel he these
  words caught,
And this figure he added also:
That if gold rusts, what shall iron do?
For if a priest be foul, in whom
  we trust,
No wonder that a coarse man
  should rust.
And a shame it is, if a priest
  ends up
A filthy shepherd with clean sheep.
Well ought a priest give an example

And shame it is, if a prest taake keep,	By his cleanness, how his sheep should live.
A shiten shepherde and a clene sheep.	
Wel oghte a prees ensample for to yive,	
By his clennesse, how that his sheep sholde lyve.[1]	

Geoffrey Chaucer lived five centuries before Bonhoeffer, during a period when the church was deeply corrupt. Chaucer saw—or imagined—one lowly, local pastor who was an exception. The description of that fourteenth century pastor fits Dietrich Bonhoeffer. Alongside Chaucer's delightful words I've appended my own translation, trying to capture the flavor but not pretending to match the genius of Chaucer.

In Dietrich Bonhoeffer, the gold did not rust. He lived the same Gospel which he taught and faithfully followed his Lord through the church into the world, through the world unto the Cross, and through death into life eternal. All by the grace of God.

Endnotes

1   Leibholz-Bonhoeffer, Sabine, *The Bonhoeffers: Portrait of a Family* (New York: Covenant Press, 1994), 175.

2   *Prayer and Righteous Action.*

3   This translation can be found on the website: http://www.history.ucsb.edu/faculty/marcuse/projects/niem/StuttgartDeclaration.htm.

4   Barnett, *For the Soul of the People*. See the whole section, 208-220.

5   Ferdinand Schlingensiepen, *Dietrich Bonhoeffer 1906-1945: Martyr, Thinker, Man of Resistance,* first German edition 2006 (New York: T & T Clark, 2010), xvii, 347

APPENDIX ONE

Timeline

Date	Bonhoeffer, Church. and Conspiracy	Writings
1906	DB born February 4 in Breslau; sixth of eight children born to a prominent psychiatrist. Both parents from ancient and aristocratic families.	
1912	Father appointed professor at Berlin University; family moves.	
1918	Brother Walter killed in trenches of France.	
1919	Chooses career in theology.	
1923	DB begins theological studies at Tübingen.	
1924	Summer in Rome and North Africa: deeply impressed by the importance of church in the life of a people. Returns to study in Berlin.	
1925	Begins reading Karl Barth and Kierkegaard.	
1927	Earns doctorate in preparation for academic career; graduation in December.	Thesis: *Communion of Saints*.
1928	Appointed intern in Barcelona in preparation for pastoral career.	Lecture: *Jesus Christ and the Essence of Christianity*.
1929	Academic Assistant at Berlin University.	Lecture in Barcelona: *Basic Questions of a Christian Ethic?* Habilitation Thesis: *Act and Being*.
1930	Qualifies for professorship; leaves for year of study as Sloan Fellow at Union Seminary in New York; finds American theology shallow but appreciates growing ethical sensitivity in America, especially through acquaintance with Black students.	
1931	Returns to Berlin, becomes friends with Barth; receives appointment as lecturer, though still not paid; drawn into international ecumenical work; ordained in November; begins involvement with ecumenical movement.	

Year	Events	Writings
1932	Lectures on Genesis.	Genesis lectures: *Creation and Fall*. Lecture: *Thy Kingdom Come*. Lecture: *The Church Is Dead*.
1933	2/1: In national radio broadcast, warns Germany of worshiping Führer above Lord. April: publishes article rejecting Hitler's ban on Jews in church; teaches summer course on Christology; works with Niemöller and others to form Pastors' Emergency League, yet is deeply discouraged by relative lack of alarm among pastors and accepts pastorate in London while rethinking his opposition, which becomes more solid than ever; Bethel Confession.	Christology lectures: reconstructed from student notes and published in 1960 as *Christ the Center*. Essay: *The Church and the Jewish Question*
1934	5/29-31: Confessing Church forms around the Barmen Confession, written mostly by Barth; Bonhoeffer tries with little success to rally international ecumenical support for Confessing Church.	
1935	4/26: Returns to Germany to lead seminary at Finkenwald for Confessing Church.	Lecture: *The Interpretation of the New Testament*. 1/35: Letter to Karl-Friedrich Bonhoeffer.
1936	Loses authorization to teach at Berlin University.	1/36: Letter to Elizabeth Zinn; 4/36: Letter to Rüdiger Schleicher.
1937	DB despairs of ecumenical movement; 3/4: Pope Pius XI issues encyclical, "With Burning Anxiety," charging Hitler with infractions of the Concordat of 1933; Gestapo closes Seminary and later arrests 27 former students; Seminary goes underground and lasts, with little effect, until early 1940.	Publication of *Discipleship*, gathering themes which had occupied his mind at least since 1928.
1938	1/11:Nazis forbid DB to work or speak in Berlin; Feb: begins work with political resistance (Canaris, Oster, Beck, Sack, Dohnanyi, etc.); lectures on "Temptation" at brief reunion of seminarians; helps his twin sister and her Jewish husband escape to England.	Writes *Life Together*, reflecting on experience of communal living.

1939	Goes to Union Seminary again but returns to Germany almost immediately because he does not want to evade sharing the cost of discipleship; has family and friends, members of the resistance, in the *Abwehr* give him an appointment so that he'll not be drafted. Joins conspiracy to kill Hitler.	
1940	Forbidden to speak in public and ordered to report regularly to police, even while carrying on life of double agent as a spy; still travels internationally on "official" business.	Begins writing *Ethics*, a task completed by Bethge.
1941	Continues international travel under guise of being a spy, seeks to persuade England that the Resistance is ready to move; Churchill is unimpressed.	
1942		Essay: *After Ten Years*.
1943	1/17: Becomes engaged; April 5: arrested for smuggling Jews out of Germany.	Writes brief letters and essays in prison, later collected by Bethge and published as *Letters and Papers from Prison*.
1944	7/20: Failed assassination attempt. A prison guard prepares to help Bonhoeffer escape, but Bonhoeffer decides against it for fear of reprisals against his family.	Writes most profound theological letters, beginning in April.
1945	4/9: Bonhoeffer and others executed by hanging at Flossenberg concentration camp. 4/23: Klaus Bonhoeffer, Rüdiger Schleicher, and others executed by firing squad. Family does not learn of deaths until June. In September, Protestant church issues the "Stuttgart Declaration," acknowledging but not specifying guilt and not mentioning Jews.	

APPENDIX TWO

A Brief Bonhoeffer Bibliography

Writings

Dietrich Bonhoeffer Works in English, Fortress Press, is an outstanding series of 17 volumes, including all of Bonhoeffer's writing, including his voluminous correspondence, books, lectures, reports, and sermons. The material is thoroughly annotated and introduced both by English and German scholars. Perhaps too extensive and expensive and extensive for most readers, it is richly rewarding for those who can devote the time and money for careful study.

   I. *Sanctorum Communio.*
   II. *Act and Being.*
   III. *Creation and Fall.*
   IV. **Discipleship.* (Formerly in English: *The Cost of Discipleship*)
   V. *Life Together and *Prayerbook of the Bible.*
   VI. **Ethics.*
   VII. *Fiction from Tegel Prison.*
   VIII. **Letters and Papers from Prison.*
   IX. *The Young Bonhoeffer, 1918–1927.*
   X. *Barcelona, Berlin, New York: 1928–1931.*
   XI. *Ecumenical, Academic and Pastoral Work: 1931–1932,*
   XII. *Berlin: 1932–1933.*
   XIII *London, 1933–1935.*
   XIV. *Theological Education at Finkenwalde: 1935–1937.*
   XV. *Theological Education Underground: 1937–1940.*
   XVI. *Conspiracy and Imprisonment 1940–1945.*

Selections from His Writings

Gracie, David, *Meditating on the Word*, Cowley Publications, 1986. Selections and sermons exemplifying Bonhoeffer's trust in and use of Scripture.

---

* An asterisk indicates especially valuable works for those becoming acquainted with Bonhoeffer and his work.

*Green, Clifford and Michael DeJonge. *The Bonhoeffer Reader*. Fortress Press, 2013. An excellent sampling of his writings, using the best translations and with excellent introductions. Designed as a "next step" after reading a biography or two but before tackling *DBWE*.

Kelly, Geffrey and Burton Nelson. *A Testament to Freedom*, 2nd ed. Harper San Francisco, 1995. A very good but older selection of excerpts. The introductions are excellent, but the translations have now been surpassed by those in *DBWE*.

Biographies

*Bethge, Eberhard. *Dietrich Bonhoeffer: Theologian, Christian, Man for His Times*. Fortress Press, 2000. This is the standard against which all others will be measured for a long time to come. The book is more than a thousand pages, all of them interesting and informative. Bethge was Bonhoeffer's closest friend and our greatest resource for knowledge of Bonhoeffer.

Metaxas, Eric. *Bonhoeffer: Pastor, Martyr, Prophet, Spy*. Thomas Nelson, 2010. Metaxas is a good storyteller but his book, while interesting, has several serious flaws. His knowledge of German history is inaccurate in a number of important details. Worse, he seems to have badly misunderstood Bonhoeffer's theology and to have failed to notice that the "death of God" theologians of the 1960s have long since been discredited and have disappeared from the scene. In an oddly Quixotic way, he battles against the "liberals," without having any idea who they are, what they represent, or how much Bonhoeffer respected them. Through a highly selective and tendencious use of sources, he unrealistically portrays Bonhoeffer as quite like a contemporary evangelical.

Raum, Elizabeth. *Dietrich Bonhoeffer, Called by God*. Bloomsbury Publishing, 2003. A research librarian, writer, and wife of a Presbyterian pastor, Raum set out to write an introduction to Bonhoeffer suitable for teens. She ended up with a readable and useful book for people of any age who are just becoming acquainted with Bonhoeffer.

*Schlingensiepen, Ferdinand, *Dietrich Bonhoeffer, 1906-1945 : Martyr, Thinker, Man of Resistance*. T & T Clark, 2010. Highly regarded by Bonhoeffer scholars, the author was a longtime friend of Eberhard Bethge, who encouraged the writing of this biography.

Biographical Fiction

Giardina, Denise. *Saints and Villains*. Norton, 1998. A well written novel which nonetheless takes too many liberties to portray Bonhoeffer as a hero on a pedestal of clay.

Glazener, Mary. *The Cup of Wrath*. Smyth & Helwys, 1996. This is the most respected of the several novels built around the life and work of Bonhoeffer.

Van Dyke, Michael. *The Story of Dietrich Bonhoeffer: Radical Integrity*. Barbour, 2001. This is a readable book but suffers from a lack of focus. It is neither as entertaining as a novel nor as informative as a biography. All the thorny problems of understanding the ideas of Bonhoeffer are deftly evaded.

Wind, Renate. *A Spoke in the Wheel*. Wm. B. Eerdmans Publishing Co., 2002. First published some twenty years earlier, this novel is liked by some but found awkward by most, primarily because of the rough translation. It is often neglected because other works share its strengths but not its weaknesses.

Background Resources

Bethge, Eberhard. *Dietrich Bonhoeffer: A Life in Pictures*. Fortress Press, 2005. A wide variety of photos of Dietrich and his historical context, with extensive and very useful annotations, though it is not a full biography.

Bethge, Eberhard and Renate. *Last Letters of Resistance*. Fortress Press, 1986. A small collection of writings from the members of the Bonhoeffer family who were executed by the Nazis.

Bonhoeffer, Sabine (Leibholz). *Portrait of a Family*. Covenant Publications, 1994. Memories of the various family members; written by Bonhoeffer's twin sister Sabine.

Introductions to Bonhoeffer's Thought

Haynes, Stephen and Lori Brandt Hale. *Bonhoeffer for Armchair Theologians*. Westminster/John Knox Press, 2009. A thoughtful examination of some of Bonhoeffer's key ideas. Especially good on connecting his work with the historical context in Nazi Germany.

Kelly, Geffrey B. and F. Burton Kelly. *The Cost of Moral Leadership: The Spirituality of Dietrich Bonhoeffer*. Wm B. Eerdmans Publishing

Co., 2003. An excellent study of the interconnectedness of morality, justice, spirituality, and discipleship.

Lawrence, Joel. *Bonhoeffer: A Guide for the Perplexed*. T & T Clark, 2010. Somewhat difficult for those not acquainted with theological issues, this book is nonetheless an excellent discussion of the basic themes of Bonhoeffer's writings. Lawrence is a pastor in St. Paul and former professor of theology at Bethel Seminary.

*Matthews, John. *Anxious Souls Will Ask: The Christ-centered Spirituality of Dietrich Bonhoeffer*. Wm. B. Eerdmans Publishing Co., 2005. An excellent introduction to some of Bonhoeffer's most challenging ideas. Matthews, a Lutheran pastor in Apple Valley, Minnesota, is a former president of the English language section of the International Bonhoeffer Society.

*Matthews, John. *Bonhoeffer: A Brief Overview of the Life and Writings of Dietrich Bonhoeffer*. Lutheran University Press, 2011. A very good look at the broad sweep of Bonhoeffer's thinking over the years, helping dispel the persistent mistake of thinking Bonhoeffer's later radical ideas were disconnected from his earlier, more "evangelical" views.

Video

Bonhoeffer. Martin Doblmeier, 2005. The best video available, with a good balance of narration, interviews, old photographs and footage, and contemporary images from Germany.

Bonhoeffer: Agent of Grace. PBS, 2000. Unfortunately, PBS seems to have allowed itself to be swayed by Hollywood's way of telling a story. The engagement of Bonhoeffer just weeks before his arrest allowed almost no time for significant contact between Bonhoeffer and Maria, yet this video seems like a love story. Worse, in order to highlight the extremely difficult situation of the prisoners being held for their conspiracy against Hitler, the director portrays Bonhoeffer as a trembling, fearful man, quite far from the calm with which he always conducted himself in the presence of any other people. Not recommended.

Hanged on a Twisted Cross. T. N. Mohan, 1996. This is a solid but rather unimaginative view of Bonhoeffer. The photographs and films of Germany in the 1930s are excellent, but the droll narration by actor

Ed Asner detracts from the effectiveness of the video.

Restless Conscience. Hava Kohav Beller, 2009. A video about the wide variety of efforts to halt or assassinate Hitler, with Bonhoeffer being only one of several brave souls featured.

Audio Drama

Bonhoeffer: The Cost of Freedom. Focus on the Family, 1997. This radio drama tells the story of Bonhoeffer while keeping a certain distance from his theology.

Online

The International Bonhoeffer Society-English Language Section maintains a website that includes events, book reviews and significant resources for ongoing Bonhoeffer studies. To access the website, go to www.thebonhoeffercenter.org.

About the Author

Dr. Michael T. Hayes spent twenty-six years pastoring churches in the Midwest, leading numerous Bible studies and focusing on discipleship. Prior to these years, he spent ten years in campus ministry as campus staff and area director with InterVarsity Christian Fellowship at the University of Hawaii, where he focused on teaching inductive Bible study, prayer, and fellowship as foundations for the students. He has a BA in psychology from Sonoma State University in California, an MDiv and DMin from Fuller Seminary. He has pursued a wide variety of studies including the Gospel of Mark, Dietrich Bonhoeffer, church history, and Western civilization. His favorite ways of spending time were being with his family, reading, listening to classical music, and enjoying the great outdoors.

Michael died on February 24, 2018, after a battle of several years against cancer. His death came only one month before the publication of this book, his labor of two decades and culmination of a lifetime of engagement with the legacy of Dietrich Bonhoeffer. Bonhoeffer's final words at Flossenburg on April 9, 1945, could well be Michael's words at Red Wing in 2018: "This is the end; for me the beginning of life." Michael, *Ruhe in Frieden*!

www.ingramcontent.com/pod-product-compliance
Lightning Source LLC
Chambersburg PA
CBHW050317120526
44592CB00014B/1945